Belief

BY THE SAME AUTHOR
Durable Solutions

Belief

How Our Minds Work (and How They Don't)

Gil Carroll

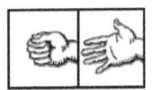

Good Reasons Press

Copyright © 2021 Gil Carroll

First Published by Good Reasons Press in 2021
www.goodreasons.co
Cover Design by Bianca Bordianu
Editing by Dale Ulland

All rights reserved, Good Reasons Press. No part of this book may be used or reproduced in any manner whatsoever without written permission from the publisher except in the case of brief quotations embodied in critical articles or reviews. For information contact Good Reasons Press, www.goodreasons.co.

Paperback ISBN 978-1-7366293-0-7
eBook ISBN 978-1-7366293-1-4

For information about Good Reasons and to
sign up for updates,
please visit www.goodreasons.co

"It is wrong always, everywhere, and for anyone, to believe anything upon insufficient evidence."
— William Kingdon Clifford

Contents

Introduction ... 1
The Run-Up to Reason ... 9
The Great Demotions ... 23
The Surge of Reason ... 39
Science ... 53
A Good Theory ... 69
The Grand Conspiracy, and Others ... 81
Going Forward ... 123

Introduction

"The highest activity a human being can attain is learning for understanding, because to understand is to be free."[1]
– Baruch Spinoza

HISTORY IS LOUSY WITH beliefs that were once commonplace but that seem absurd today. These include the beliefs that fairies live in the woods (as do leprechauns); that there exist witches who have sex with demons in the forest at midnight (we should find these witches and burn them); that worms are created when rainwater mixes with dirt; that leaving wrapped bread and cheese in a dark corner will create mice; that fleas come from dust and maggots from rotting meat; and that human sperm look like little people.

Also, Earth is flat, and the sun, the moon and the heavens orbit around it; telescopes and microscopes are tools that trick the senses and should not be trusted; and garlic neutralizes magnets. Heavy objects fall faster than lighter objects; seeing happens when our eyes shine invisible rays on objects; malaria comes from bad air; travel by train can cause insanity; if people travel faster than the speed of sound, they will die; and space travel will puncture holes in the atmosphere that will let the air to leak out.

To say modern people are more intelligent than past generations would be simplistic and self-serving. However, it is true that humans have changed considerably over the past five centuries regarding how we construct our beliefs. We have also adopted a few ways whereby we can scrutinize our beliefs.

If we choose to, that is.

We are comfortable assuming that our beliefs are correct, and so we feel no need to scrutinize them. This is unfortunate, as the bias we have to favor our own beliefs is a bug and not a feature. Some beliefs are better than others. Some beliefs are more harmful than others. As described in the phrase "He who would own a monkey should pay for the glasses it breaks," we are responsible for the damage caused by our bad beliefs.

Do we hold any beliefs today that will seem eccentric or quaint – or even shameful – to our descendants?

Should you feed a cold and starve a fever? Spread butter over a burn? Pee on a jellyfish sting? My friend's son thinks that turning on the porch-light causes the sun to set.

Is the world run by a few secret organizations such as the Illuminati and the Dead Bones Society? Are these organizations conspiring to implement a New World Order that nobody knows about (except, of course, those fortunate people who do). Some claim this NWO will take power after it causes a global economic collapse, possibly triggered by the COVID-19 pandemic, possibly with the assistance of 5G-network technology. Some say the United Nations is a witting participant in this conspiracy, and therefore we should suspect their intentions and their actions.

At one time, people believed that the atmosphere contained a mysterious element called ether. Today, we say the universe is full of "dark matter," stuff we can neither see nor measure directly. Some believe that the

Large Hadron Collider in Europe – used to smash particles into one another at super high speeds – could open up a black hole that might suck Earth in.

Is the gift of speaking in tongues real? Does God really care if we eat pork or help refugees? Does the Bible predict the future of the United States?

Is DNA research real science? What about gene editing? Magnetic bracelets? Does hypnosis work? Do vaccinations cause autism? Can people become possessed? Does the pyramid shape emit energy? Does quantum theory have spiritual implications?

Some people believe Earth is heating up at an unprecedented rate that will cause devastating destruction and possibly even mass extinction. Some believe that human activity is to blame for this warming. Others dismiss climate change as just a natural fluctuation or possibly even a Chinese hoax.

Is being gay a circumstance that can – and should – be cured?

Did Bill and Hillary Clinton have John F. Kennedy Jr. killed? Some people believe that if you fall off a cliff, you will die of shock before you hit the ground. Some believe Barack Obama is really a Kenyan-born Muslim, and others believe he is neither Kenyan-born nor Muslim; rather, they believe, he was born in Hawaii. Some think the world ended in 1914 – or 1978 – or in 2000, but few noticed its demise because it ended only on a spiritual level. Some believe we are now in the end times. Some say 9/11 was an inside job. Others think belief in evolution will lead to atheism and communism.

Many people in the 1930s thought that water that

had been made radioactive was a health drink. Today, some people say Kombucha is healthful.

Our beliefs ultimately lead to policy. For example, some see the growth in human population as a major threat. Others think that making birth control or abortion widely available is an even worse threat. Some people think that race is real, and that brain size and skin color influence intelligence and therefore we should take special care how we organize society.

It is not only the odd stuff people believe that should concern us. A bigger problem might be the true things that we do not believe. Will our descendants consider our hesitancy to take climate change seriously the ultimate act of irresponsibility? Will we hand them a world without polar bears, hippopotamuses and snow?

This book is about belief. We will discuss the various ways through which we arrive at a belief: Reason, tradition, intuition, prejudice, authority, observation and experiment – they all play a role in determining how we believe. Ideally, we establish our beliefs upon good reasons and guard against the many ways we can fall prey to bad beliefs.

Chapter 1, titled "The Run-Up to Reason," begins with a brief discussion about the process of making sense of the world as it worked before the massive changes brought by the Protestant Reformation and the Scientific Revolution. In Chapter 2, "The Great Demotions," we discuss the adjustments to the various paths to truth that sprang from these changes. Chapter 3, "The Surge of Reason," concerns the paths to truth that emerged as other paths declined, including the rising primacy of the fact. Chapter 4, "Science," discusses the development of science and why it has had such a significant impact on the way society gathers knowledge. In Chapter 5, "A Good Theory," we drill down on the scientific way we approach an issue and discuss why the process of developing a sound theory is critical to the reasoning process. Chapter 6, "The Grand Conspiracy, the Super-Spreader of Poor Thinking," discusses the many ways a non-critical mind can stray from the path of reason. Finally, in Chapter 7, "Going Forward," we suggest ways to ensure that our thinking stays rigorous. My hope is that readers will gain an understanding of the historical events that led to the modern belief process; that there still are traps that can compromise human reasoning; and that there are steps we can take to ensure that we do not fall victim to these traps.

Why Is belief important?

Beliefs are inevitable

Humans cannot help but organize reality into categories of belief. That's what we do. We symbolize. We rationalize. We defend. We are constantly creating arguments and defending them in our internal chatter – our self-talk. We then express them externally to our family, friends and community. We construct reality filters and starting points of discussion. Next, we draw patterns that simplify and generalize, and we construct bulwarks from which we defend our beliefs.

We cannot avoid participating in this organizing

process, and in this sense we are all scientists, albeit probably we are poorer scientists than we could be. Our brains are always organization machines, but they are not always unbiased and consistent reasoning machines.

Beliefs have consequences

While we have no control over whether we organize reality, we do have control over how skillfully we do it. "The essence of the independent mind," said author Christopher Hitchens, "lies not in what it thinks, but in how it thinks."[2] We have control over the degree to which we draw our beliefs from authority and tradition; the degree to which we fall prey to comforting prejudice, cognitive traps and logical fallacies; and the degree to which we apply skeptical reasoning and humility toward our beliefs.

If the ability to reason is what sets humans apart from other animals, then we have an interest in leveraging reason as best we can. Galileo Galilei, the most famous case of an individual choosing observation over authority, said, "I do not feel obliged to believe that the same God who has endowed us with sense, reason and intellect has intended us to forgo their use."[3]

Our beliefs determine how we structure our lives. They determine our religious orientation, our political ideals and associations, our consumer appetites and behavior, our romantic preferences, and our short-term and long-term goals. Beliefs also determine how – and whether – we enter into the corrective discussions that ensure that also our beliefs are reasonable. Beliefs not only determine what will occupy our minds, but they fuel what we do and don't do. Our beliefs inform our days, months and years, eventually determining how we live our lives. Therefore, we should take care that they are formed responsibly, with care and intention.

Beliefs bubble up to form collective versions of reality

We have hygienic responsibility not only over our physical health, but also over our epistemic health. We create hygienic systems that ensure our physical health while protecting others from the consequences of our hygienic neglect, such as the spread of harmful disease. Our intellectual hygiene is equally important. Intellectual hygiene not only helps ensure that our own reasoning is sound, but also protects others from the consequences of our poor reasoning, such as the spread of harmful beliefs.

Beliefs are susceptible to all sorts of deceptions

The sun revolves around Earth. The king is God's representative on Earth. Slavery is the natural order. Mice spontaneously generate from straw. Each of these beliefs was at one time commonly accepted. Evolutionary theory, climate change and immigration are divisive issues of our day. Wherever we land on these issues, we want to ensure that our conclusions are supported by good reasons – that we are not simply accepting comfortable beliefs from past traditions and authorities, current passions, prejudices and unchecked intuitions, just as human beings have done throughout history.

Well-founded beliefs are necessary in a democracy.

Especially in a democracy, if the thinking process of voters is sloppy, we can expect that our government, too, will be sloppy. As our beliefs solidify, and we associate more with like-minded people, and together we pursue agendas about every aspect of our lives. Socrates named the loss of critical thinking as the greatest danger to both society and to the individual.[4] Ultimately, this determines the health – or sickness – of our community, our nation and our world. More than with other governments, a democratically elected one reflects the thoughts of the people that it represents.

CHAPTER ONE

The Run-Up to Reason

The Preponderance of Authority

"This council declares that if anyone disagrees with it, they are damned."[1]
— Council of Trent, Canon 33, 1547

THROUGHOUT MUCH OF WESTERN history, certainly before the Protestant Reformation in the 16th century and the Scientific Revolution in the following one, the Catholic Church was the primary source of authority regarding matters of faith. The Church also spoke on matters of the physical world because the separation between the spiritual and the natural was not as clear as it is today. (Indeed, the word "scientist" did not even exist until the 18th century.) Natural philosophy was the science of the day. The Church also co-opted the authority of some of the ancients –

including Plotinus and Aristotle – in order to buttress Scripture and to provide a secular entry into non-Christian cultures. Other ways of knowing such as personal faith, direct observation, philosophy, reason, intuition, emotion and commonsense were used to elucidate – not challenge – the basic narrative of the Church.

As Yuval Noah Harari points out in his book "Sapiens: A Brief History of Humankind," the Church was authoritative on not just what people needed to believe, but also what sort of questions were even worth asking. Harari said:

> [If we] wanted to know how spiders weave their webs, it was pointless to ask the priest, because there was no answer to this question in any of the Christian Scriptures. That did not mean, however, that Christianity was deficient. Rather, it meant that understanding how spiders weaved their webs was unimportant.[2]

If the Church did not have an answer, the question was probably not worth asking.

Even philosophy during that time was generally a tool used to elucidate truths that came from Scripture. Consider the geocentric theory, which is the one proposed by Ptolemy in the 1st century that claimed all the heavens orbited Earth. The geocentric theory was consistent with the biblical narrative. Other theories about the natural world that fit the narrative less well were either marginalized or labeled as pagan.

Today, we hear the common refrain from Bible

apologists that the Bible is not a science book. Before the development of a natural science, however, the Bible was a science book, or at least it was treated as one. In the absence of a robust and distinct study of science, the Bible was one of the closest things to a science that people had. The Bible was a starting point from which to organize the universe, and natural philosophy from other sources was pressed into a role that was subservient to the biblical narrative that says God placed humanity at the center of creation. Martin Luther argued that Scripture is the final authority in understanding nature:

> There is talk of a new astrologer [Nicolaus Copernicus] who wants to prove that the earth moves and goes around instead of the sky, the sun, the moon, just as if somebody were moving in a carriage or ship might hold that he was sitting still and at rest while the earth and the trees walked and moved. But that is how things are nowadays: when a man wishes to be clever he must needs invent something special, and the way he does it must needs be the best! The fool wants to turn the whole art of astronomy upside-down. However, as Holy Scripture tells us, so did Joshua bid the sun to stand still and not the earth.[3]

The job of philosophy was not to ask whether a proclamation made by biblical authorities was true, but rather what were the implications of this truth that was gleaned from Scripture. David Wootton, author of "The Invention of Science," writes, "If people generally believe that mice are spontaneously generated in straw, then the task of the philosopher is to explain why this is so, not whether it is so."[4] Scripture remained the authority with which we developed philosophy and reason, and in this relationship there was little adversarial tension. The Church had little interest in reasoning that did not support official Church doctrine. All the times when reason seemed to present a potential divergence from faith, the doctrine of the Church retained primacy.

These centuries saw slow, incremental improvements of small technologies gained through the ingenuity of craftsmen, but nothing on a scale that would challenge the authority of the Church. However, this was about to change, as the invention of the printing press and an increasing literacy began to spread in the West.

The 14th century witnessed the first of two successive challenges to ecclesiastical authority. The first was the challenge, which came from the Protestant Reformation about the Church's authority to speak definitively on spiritual matters. The second came with the Scientific Revolution, which challenged the Church's authority to speak authoritatively on matters of the natural world.

Together, these two forces introduced stress points that have plagued the Church ever since. They posed fundamental questions that still are relevant today: Are there passages of the Bible that, while they may point to a large truth, are not literally true? If so, which parts? Which parts describe the natural world? Which parts were never intended to be taken literally?

Superstition

"Superstition is to religion what astrology is to astronomy: the mad daughter of a wise mother."[1]
— Voltaire

We should spend a moment talking about another force on which people were relying in their efforts to make sense of the world: superstition. An estimated total of 40,000-50,000 people were executed as witches in the 15th, 16th and 17th centuries. Historians agree that this was probably due to a surplus of superstition and not to a surplus of witches. Historian Will Durant writes that superstition had then, as it does now, a wide appeal across society:

> Even in a widely prosperous country – and especially among the harassed poor and the idle rich – thought has to live in a jungle of superstitions: astrology, numerology, palmistry, portents, the evil eye, witches, goblins, ghosts, demons, incantations, exorcisms, dream interpretations, oracles, miracles, quackery, and occult qualities, curative or injurious, in minerals, plants, and animals. ...To the poor in body and mind superstition is a treasured element in the poetry of life.[2]

What role does superstition play in religion? Some say that superstition is the fearful underside of religion, a "vain fear of the Gods," said Cicero, whereas religion was a "pious adoration of them."[3] "The Great Agnostic," Robert Green Ingersoll, was not so generous.

Ingersoll said that superstition is the "mother of those hideous twins, Fear and Faith, [which] from her throne of skulls, still rules the world."[4] The 19th century author James Fenimore Cooper said, "Ignorance and superstition ever bear a close and mathematical relation to each other."[5] Is superstition the religion for the uneducated and weak-minded? Superstition decreases as education increases, notes philosopher and author Richard Carrier:

> The first thing that strikes any student of antiquity is how the miraculous was so strangely common then, yet became less and less common as literacy, education and science spread, until today when it is nowhere to be found but in urban legends, obscure backwaters, and other suspicious circumstances.[6]

Evolutionary biologist Jerry Coyne, author of the book "Faith vs. Fact," said that superstition is not just the weak underbelly of religion, but that religion is itself a form of superstition: "Religion is but a single brand of superstition (others include beliefs in astrology, paranormal phenomena, homeopathy, and spiritual healing), but it is the most widespread and harmful form of superstition."[7]

Wherever people come down on the issue, they generally agree that an excess of superstition does not coincide with an excess of reason.

The Reformation

"I am more afraid of my own heart than of the pope and all his cardinals. I have within me the great pope, Self."[1]
— Martin Luther

The church reformation movement under Martin Luther in circa 1519 was by no means the first challenge to the authority of the Catholic Church. The 14th century also witnessed challenges and competitions. Critics complained that the Catholic clergy considered themselves a privileged class. Critics complained that the clergy were rich, hypocritical and unconcerned about the poor. Further, the Church claimed a sole divine right to curate, translate, interpret and disseminate sacred Scripture. The official Catholic translation of the Bible was the 4th-century Latin Vulgate. Church liturgy was delivered in Latin, even though the language was not commonly understood by anyone other than clerics and scholars.

In the years leading up to his death, John Wycliffe, an outspoken early critic of the Church and advocate of the poor, finished translating an English version of the Bible. Wycliffe called into question the biblical justification for the papacy and for the Church. He called for the divestment of all Church property. Wycliffe died of natural causes in 1384. However, the Church deemed him a heretic and had his remains exhumed and burned 34 years after his death.

In 1415, another critic of the Catholic Church, Jan Has, was burned at the stake for his accusations of Catholic overreach, mismanagement and the Catholic claim to exclusive authority to interpret Scripture.

By 1519, the fruit of revolution had ripened. What made Martin Luther successful in a centuries-old movement, while his predecessors Wycliffe, Has and others saw only limited success? Technology is one answer. Technology in the form of the printing press, which was invented in 1440, allowed Luther to run what is sometimes referred to as the first mass-media campaign in history. Mario Livio, in his book "Galileo and the Science Deniers," wrote,

> As an early precursor to e-mail, Twitter, Instagram, and Facebook, printing also allowed individuals to transmit their ideas to the masses more rapidly and efficiently. When the German theologian Martin Luther campaigned for church reform, he was assisted greatly by the existence of printing. In particular, his translation of the Bible from Latin into German vernacular, to represent his ideal of a world in which ordinary people could consult the word of God for themselves, had a profound impact on both the modern German language and the Church in general. About two hundred thousand copies in hundreds of reprinted editions appeared before Luther's death.[2]

As is the case with all inventions that enhance communication – such as the radio, television and the internet – the printing press provided more information but not necessarily better information. This movement was not really motivated by the love of reason as we define it today. Reason was still largely a servant of faith, and basis of faith was to be found in Holy

Scripture. Of faith and reason, faith remained the foundation of the two.

Similarly, philosophy remained unconcerned with the veracity of Church truths, but only with the implications of these truths. The conflict of the Reformation was not over whether Scripture was authoritative, but over who had the authority to interpret Scripture: the Catholic Church, or other Christian churches or even the individual worshipper. In these cases, importantly, it was the authority of the Church, and not the authority of Scripture, that was questioned.

Astronomy Shaming

"All philosophies that assume a central role of humanity in the universe spring from self-importance, and are best corrected by a little astronomy."[3]
— Bertrand Russell

It is easy to think that all human advancement has been a steady, slow progression through time. But really, the end of the 16th century and throughout the 17th century – the period around the Scientific Revolution – witnessed an amazing acceleration in the ability to observe, understand and collect information about the natural world.

Regarding the visible world, for instance, the telescope revealed an expansive heaven in a detail never before seen, filled with objects following trajectories totally independent of Earth. At the other extreme, the microscope revealed that a drop of water contained swarms of life forms, busy with their own processes.

The impact of these tools that extended human senses cannot be overstated. Before the appearance of these tools, people largely were unaware that their perceptions were limited, and so the assumption was that the world consisted of only what raw human senses could perceive.

Once these tools began to show that there may be more than meets the eye, a crisis – one of trust – appeared. Could these tools be trusted to provide an accurate view of the natural world? To determine this, people needed to study how these tools worked to enhance, not trick, our senses. As these studies progressed, scientists obtained a better understanding of how our senses work. Could our other senses – sound, taste, touch and smell – be similarly enhanced?

Visual tools such as the telescope and the microscope presented a way of seeing that had not previously existed, and consequently they were met with great skepticism, suspicion and hesitation. This was especially true when the information these tools revealed ran counter to official Church explanations, in which cases they also challenged Church authority. Laura J. Snyder, author of "Eye of the Beholder: Johannes Vermeer, Antoni van Leeuwenhoek, and the Reinvention of Seeing," said that these tools redefined what it meant to see:

> The widespread acceptance of optical instruments in science required not only optical theories explaining how they worked, but also – and especially – the

willingness to accept that there is more than meets the eye. That the world is not simply the way it appears to us. Behind the phenomena we see with the naked eye is an unseen world. And in this invisible world, lie the causes of the natural processes we observe.[4]

Acceptance that the natural world was much bigger – and also much smaller – than people had assumed forced a change in perspective that is still being reckoned with today. This realization challenged the belief in human centrality in creation, and also to the confidence that had up until now been placed in the reliability of human intuitions. Of the period, Durant said:

> The eyes could not see clearly enough, far enough, minutely enough; the flesh could not feel with requisite accuracy the pressure, warmth, and weight of things; the mind could not measure space, time, quantity, quality, density without mingling its personal equation with the facts. Microscopes were needed, telescopes, thermometers, barometers, hydrometers, better watches, finer scales. One by one they came.[5]

These instruments proved disruptive to common categories of knowledge and understanding, calling into question long-accepted truths. Long-ensconced assumptions could now be tested through tools such as the telescope, and potentially people could each determine their own understanding of reality. What previously had been underutilized categories of knowing – including evidence and direct observation – were now being reevaluated and were taking center stage, whereas other categories such as tradition were also being reevaluated, albeit in the other direction.

Church authority was now challenged on two fronts: first with the Reformation of the mid-16th century and then from a natural philosophy perspective with the Scientific Revolution. For example, the sun, as seen through an extension of the telescope called the helioscope (this device projected the sun's image onto a piece of paper, so observers were able to look at the sun without damaging their eyes), was not the pristine orb symbolic of divine perfection as had been long thought. Rather, these instruments revealed that the sun appeared to contain blemishes, or "sun-spots." Nor was the moon pure – apparently, it was replete with mountains and craters.

Furthermore, the number of known planets – which had been thought to be an example of the biblically significant number "seven" – was also seemingly incorrect, as more heavenly objects were regularly being discovered. Jupiter even appeared to have objects that were orbiting it, moons that seemingly cycled independently of Earth.

Finally, the sun, not Earth, increasingly was looking like it was the hub of our system, contradicting the geocentric theory that the Church had advocated for centuries.

Hoping to end this challenge to its authority once and for all, the Church's reaction to this growing Copernican, sun-centered, heliocentric "problem" was firm and severe. Perhaps aware of this tension,

Copernicus refrained from publishing his observation-rich treatise until 1542, shortly before his death. This Copernican view was later adopted by Giordano Bruno. In 1600, Bruno was hung upside down and burned at the stake for espousing this and other beliefs considered heretical. Still, the Copernican model continued to gain traction.

Galileo formally published his support of the Copernican model in the early 1600s, midway through his career. He also paid a price: Galileo's work was passed on to the inquisition in 1615, and he was personally censured. Later, in the 1630s, he was compelled to recant his views under the implied threat of torture. (As a way to cool his astronomical fever, Galileo was given a tour of the torture facilities.) Galileo watered down his rhetoric, explaining that he had overstated his observations. Even so, he spent the rest of his life under house arrest.

The Telescope and the Age of Tools

"O telescope, instrument of much knowledge, more precious than any sceptre!"[6]
— Johannes Kepler

The most significant of these new tools was the telescope. Invented in 1608, the telescope was the most noteworthy of the new instruments that allowed people to observe nature with a precision never before seen. Also, the telescope was unfamiliar and strange and, as we said, exemplified a new concept of extending our natural senses by artificial means.

So suspicious were some people toward this new "looking glass" that some professors and members of the clergy refused even to look through the eyepiece, fearing that it was a tool of deception, or perhaps even a device of the devil. Indeed, part of Galileo's challenge was to popularize this tool. He gifted telescopes to people in power, such as those from the monarchy and the merchant class. These people marveled at being able to see approaching ocean ships through the telescope's eyepiece before their unaided eyes could spot them. Galileo explained that he had only pointed this tool upward to examine the heavens. (Incidentally, the telescope first used by Galileo had a magnification of about 8x, compared with the 4700x magnification of the current Hubble telescope, which has its starting point in space, beyond the "noise" of Earth's atmosphere!)

Another technology at work, the printing press, had already been fueling another revolution, empowering individuals to read and interpret Scripture independently of the Church. Both the printing press and the telescope worked to make information more egalitarian. With the help of these tools, anyone had the potential to test the pronouncements of the Church using their own wits and the wits of others.

The implications of this new way of knowing were disruptive and disorienting to the established order, which was both dazzled and conflicted about the legitimacy of these developments.

CHAPTER TWO
The Great Demotions

Level Setting

"The eclectic is a philosopher who, trampling underfoot prejudice, tradition, antiquity, general agreement, authority – in a word, everything that controls the minds of the common herd – dares to think for himself."[1]
— Denis Diderot

IN CARL SAGAN'S 1994 book, "Pale Blue Dot: A Vision of the Human Future in Space," the astronomer lists a set of humbling adjustments to how humans consider their place in nature. Sagan said that "self-congratulatory chauvinisms" have yielded to a "series of Great Demotions, down-lifting experiences, demonstrations of our apparent insignificance, wounds that science has, in its search for Galileo's facts, delivered to human pride."[2] These demotions included not just our physical place in the universe, but several other ways we have set ourselves above other animals as unique and privileged.

This Chapter will discuss some of these demotions and the consequent readjustment of the various paths to knowledge that followed.

The Centrality of Humans: Anthropocentrism

"The biggest enemy we face is anthropocentrism. This is that common attitude that everything on this Earth was put here for [human] use."[3]
— Eric Pianka

Why did this disagreement over the position of Earth in the universe – which is of little debate today – loom so large during the 17th century? Part of the answer certainly is that Earth's place at the center of creation gave credence to the idea that humans were the reason for creation. The declaration that Earth is at the physical center of the universe or that humans inhabit the center of creation is not explicitly declared in the Bible. However, the Bible implies it, and so the Church assumed it. Yet, since that period, astronomy has consistently piled up contrary data. The idea that Earth is located at the center of the universe seemed increasingly more like a case of Earth chauvinism – a prejudice or a poetic flourish – than it did a literal cosmological statement. Not only is Earth not the center of the universe, but neither is the sun, which is only a minor star in the 100 billion stars in our galaxy, which in turn is only one of the billions of galaxies in the known universe.

In our day, the theory of evolution calls into question the biblical account that a single, special act of creation produced human beings. The degree to which this account in the Book of Genesis is literal or poetic is debated today, just as is the question of which of the terms "creation" and "universe" is more appropriate, since "creation" assumes a creator. Charles Darwin wrote, "Man in his arrogance thinks himself a great work, worthy of the interposition of a deity. More humble, and I believe truer, to consider him created from animals."[4]

Far from being the centerpiece and culmination of creation, humankind increasingly seemed merely an inessential – albeit extraordinary – participant in a much more expansive story being played out on a much larger stage and in a much larger time frame.

Earth has existed for billions of years, not the thousands of years as had been thought and taught. In fact, Earth seems to have existed for about a billion years even before it hosted life, and then billions of years before it hosted human beings. Clearly, the universe is much older than Earth, which is much older than life, and life on Earth is much older than humanity.

The estimates of the size of the universe increased at each turn, beginning with the inability to see any parallax for stars. Parallax is the phenomenon that objects shift their apparent position according to the movement of and the distance from the viewer. The nearer the object, the greater the parallax. Measuring devices at the time were unable to detect any parallax with the stars, indicating that stars are very far away. This was noted even in the 17th century, through

Galileo's telescope. The moon, sun and planets showed themselves to be closer to Earth than were the stars.

Soon, this demotion brought about by the telescope over the accuracy of our senses was made apparent on a microscopic scale. Before the invention of the microscope, human beings were unaware of the vast majority of living things on Earth – single-celled animals such as bacteria, algae, protozoa, fungi and amoebae. These animals comprise nearly all the life on our planet. Biology, microbiology, paleontology, astronomy, genetics and astrophysics all show that human beings, at least on any measurable level, do not hold a special position in creation.

We do well to remember that this period witnessed a major challenge to the notion of human self-importance. The presumption of "Humanity is the centerpiece of the universe" gave way to "Humanity is merely king of the half acre." Whereas once we seemed to be the pinnacle of earthly creation – and probably of all creation – new discoveries about the immensity of time, the vastness of space and the smallness of matter informed us that our unaided senses, intuitions and chauvinisms worked partly to limit our understanding of nature. Historian Will Durant said, "Slowly we cease to be the center and summit of the universe. Life narrows down from a spiritual drama to a biological episode."[5] And yet, as with an infant, we still prefer to think that everything is here for us.

The Centrality of Humans:
Anthropomorphism

"Is man one of God's blunders, or is God one of man's blunders?"[1]
— Friedrich Nietzsche

It is not uncommon – in fact, it is common – to assign our human attributes to non-human beings, including endowing our gods with human attributes of their own. Hundreds of years ago, the Dutch philosopher Baruch Spinoza noted that it is natural to view ourselves as the base-line context and the ideal for creation. Spinoza said:

> I believe that, if a triangle could speak, it would say, in like manner, that God is eminently triangular, while a circle would say that the divine nature is eminently circular. Thus each would ascribe to God its own attributes, would assume itself to be like God, and look on everything else as ill-shaped.[2]

The ancient Egyptian, Greek and Roman gods all possessed human characteristics. They all contended with human emotions and fell victim to human frailties. Here we find another prejudice: human chauvinism. We tend to apply our human attributes to other things. Carl Sagan said we "seem compelled to project our own nature onto Nature."[3] For example:

> Children's stories and cartoons make animals dress in clothes, live in houses, use knives and forks, and

speak. The three bears sleep in beds. The owl and the pussycat go to sea in a beautiful pea-green boat. Dinosaur mothers cuddle their young. Pelicans deliver the mail. Dogs drive cars. A worm catches a thief. Pets have human names. Dolls, nutcrackers, cups, and saucers dance and have opinions. The dish runs away with the spoon. In the Thomas the Tank Engine series, we even have anthropomorphic locomotives and railway cars, charmingly portrayed. No matter what we're thinking about, animate or inanimate, we tend to invest it with human traits. We can't help ourselves. The images come readily to mind. Children are clearly fond of them.[4]

In the 19th century, evolutionary theory questioned whether man – far from being the ultimate expression of God's creation – was really just a single branch of an overgrown and meandering evolutionary tree where extinction is common and survival is rare. Humans are actually just one type of primate. As such, humanity's continued existence no longer seemed a foregone conclusion, as had been assumed. In the "Descent of Man" (1871), Darwin wrote:

> We must, however, acknowledge, as it seems to me, that man with all his noble qualities, with sympathy which feels for the most debased, with benevolence which extends not only to other men but to the humblest living creature, with his god-like intellect which has penetrated into the movements and constitution of the solar system – with all these exalted powers – Man still bears in his bodily frame the indelible stamp of his lowly origin.[5]

Darwin noted that this human chauvinism was apparent even in the way we order human beings in nature: "If man had not been his own classifier, he would never have thought of founding a separate order for his own reception."[6] Richard Dawkins addressed this when he said, "We admit that we are like apes, but we seldom realize that we are apes."[7]

This prejudice cuts both ways. It is comforting to view ourselves as special in nature, and we generously confer our best traits to other animals and even to inanimate objects. In recent decades, we have learned that many of the qualities that we thought were ours alone – qualities such as reason, empathy, justice, a sense of the future, imagination, theory of self, the ability to use symbols, and even mathematics – are shared across the animal kingdom. Anthropologist Jane Goodall said:

> Chimpanzees, more than any other living creature, have helped us to understand that there is no sharp line between humans and the rest of the animal kingdom. It's a very blurry line, and it's getting more blurry all the time.[8]

Today, we are seeing a growing movement that pushes to expand the definition of "person" to include animals such as dolphins, apes, elephants and whales. The Non-Human Rights Project promotes the idea that habeas corpus, the legal principle that protects against unlawful imprisonment, should be extended to these animals. Court decisions in recent years have deemed at least an orangutan, a couple of chimpanzees, and an elephant as "non-human persons."[9] If this strikes you as especially absurd, remember that data are often not intuitive and now you know how geocentrists felt 500 years ago! Early last century, naturalist John Muir wrote, "The world, we are told, was made especially for man – a presumption not supported by all the facts."[10] He added:

> From the dust of the earth, from the common elementary fund, the Creator has made Homo sapiens. From the same material he has made every other creature, however noxious and insignificant to us. They are earth-born companions and our fellow mortals.[11]

The difference between humans and nonhumans is more a function of degree than it is of type. After all, humans share more than 95% of their DNA with chimpanzees. We might guard ourselves against having what anthropologist Jared Diamond called "a one-sided and self-congratulatory view of our uniqueness."[12]

Armed with our tendency to see ourselves as "apart" from the rest of creation, rather than "a part" of creation, we have given ourselves license to exploit – to the point of extinction – other animals and their habitats. Our uniqueness is perhaps coming down to the fact that we alone are "clever" enough to destroy our animal companions, our own species and possibly even our own planet.

Authority Gets a Demotion

"One of the great commandments of science is, 'Mistrust arguments from authority.'... Too many such arguments have proved too painfully wrong. Authorities must prove their contentions like everybody else."[1]
— Carl Sagan

The motto of the famous Royal Society (The Royal Society of London for Improving Natural Knowledge), founded in 1660, is directed specifically at authority: *Nullius in verba* means "Take no one's word." The rallying cry "See for yourself!" testified that careful, direct observation, sometimes with the aid of tools that extended our senses, was describing the natural world with a degree of accuracy, precision and agility that Church authorities could not.

Before the development of these tools, precise and accurate observations rarely played a role in efforts to understand the natural world. In addition, the Church had shown itself unreceptive to explanations of natural phenomena that ran counter to its already-established dogmas. New arguments were evaluated mostly on their ability to support the current paradigm, rather than on their evidential merits. To keep from attracting unwanted Church attention, observations that ran contrary to Church dogmas often were cautiously presented merely as "thought experiments," meant only to start a discussion and not as literal descriptions of reality. Mario Livio said,

> Galileo based his convictions on experimental

evidence (sometimes real, sometimes in the form of 'thought experiments' – thinking through the consequences of a hypothesis) and theoretical contemplation, and not on authority.[2]

However, data that came from the careful application of mathematics and direct observation continued to accumulate. As direct observational data was used more and more to understand the physical world, scriptural authority began to take second position. Experimentalists were becoming increasingly skeptical of Church presumption that it could speak about the natural world using Scripture as its authority.

This skepticism coincided with an increased challenge to the authority of ancient figures such as Aristotle. Revered widely simply as "the Philosopher," up until this time Aristotle had been an almost-sacred authority for traditional explanations of the natural world. But, as Bertrand Russell said, "Practically every advance in science, in logic, or in philosophy has had to be made in the teeth of opposition from Aristotle's disciples."[3]

Faith gets a Demotion

"I beg you, reject antiquity, tradition, faith, and authority! Let us begin anew by doubting everything we assume has been proven!"[4]
— Giordano Bruno

Along with this challenge to the role of authority in developing beliefs came a reevaluation of the role of faith. Faith before the Protestant Reformation can be viewed largely as a Catholic enterprise. In fact, up until the Reformation, the terms "faith" and "Catholic faith" were essentially synonymous. Faith largely meant the extent to which a person recognized and adhered to Catholic dogma. And since at the time there were no robust or systematized ways with which to study the natural world, faith and natural philosophy dovetailed comfortably together. Consequently, the job of the philosopher was simply to explore this unity between Scripture and nature in order to elucidate Church doctrine.

This relationship, however, was getting more uncomfortable for two reasons. One reason sprang from the Reformation, when reform-minded Christians were challenging the Catholic idea of faith and whether a single Church alone could define faith. Reformers were promoting the doctrine of *sola fide*, the idea that worshippers were justified by faith alone – that is by the individual, not by the determinations of a human organization such as the Catholic Church. As Robert Green Ingersoll said, the Reformation "took power from the pulpit and divided it among the pews."[5]

Importantly, the source of faith itself had not changed. The source of faith still was the Christian God of the Bible, as revealed in Holy Scripture. The challenge, rather, had more to do with who held the authority to deliver faith pronouncements: Church clerics or worshippers themselves.

The second challenge to faith came from new discoveries that brought new questions about whether faith was an effective tool with which to understand the natural world. Perhaps faith was specifically a tool of transcendence, used to aid in spiritual understanding, and less valuable as a tool with which to discover nature. We further discuss this change in Chapter 3, in the section "Laws of Nature vs. Natural law."

Religion and Philosophy Part Ways

"My dear Kepler, what would you say of the learned here, who, replete with the pertinacity of the asp, have steadfastly refused to cast a glance through the telescope? What shall we make of this? Shall we laugh, or shall we cry?"[6]
— Galileo Galilei

As faith entered this reevaluation period, the positions of religion and natural philosophy as paths to truth also were disrupted. Religion remained firmly rooted in traditional and literary authorities, whereas natural philosophy was increasingly influenced by direct observation. Religion looked back, and natural philosophy looked forward. Mario Livio noted the progression from religion to philosophy to science concerning which was best suited to address the larger questions of humanity. He wrote "A few of the most fundamental questions that humans have ever posed, have crossed, over the millennia, first the boundary between religion and philosophy, and later, the border between philosophy and science.[7]"

Leading this crossing of boundaries was the controversy between the heliocentric and geocentric world views, which had threatened from the background for centuries. Rather than adjust and adapt to these new observation-driven descriptions of the heavens that seemingly were at odds with traditional biblical explanations, the Church dug in its heels, defending its traditional interpretations of Scripture. The Church dismissed these observation-driven explanations that contradicted Church explanations of nature as rebellious man-sized answers to God-sized questions. Galileo came down on the side of observational experimentation, declaring that "all truths are easy to understand once they are discovered; the point is to discover them."[8]

Common Sense gets a Demotion

"Common sense is what tells us the earth is flat."[9]
— Stuart Chase

Common sense – the notion that reasonable people are able to accurately make sense of slices of reality – is used when we try to impose order on a new set of phenomena by comparing it to an older, familiar set of phenomena. Common sense relies on a shared base of experience, and on analogy, which largely is how the brain makes sense of things. We try to explain the unfamiliar by comparing it to the familiar.

Common sense is just that: common. However, common sense is not always accurate. Albert Einstein dismissed common sense as the "collection of prejudices acquired by age eighteen."[10] In areas where no good analogy can be made, common sense will try to force an analogy anyway. This can lead to "inside the box" thinking when "outside the box" thinking may be more appropriate. Its comparisons can be incomplete and simplistic.

For example, early astronomers had difficulty explaining the orbits of objects because they assumed that – because the universe was created by a perfect God – objects should orbit in perfect circles. But the observations about planetary orbits made over the years increasingly questioned this view. In 1609, Johannes Kepler published his "New Astronomy," in which he argued that these objects did not orbit in perfect circles, but followed elliptical orbits around the sun, where their speeds varied. In this instance, the commonsense assumption about the heavens and perfect circles was not accurate. Indeed, it actually obstructed more accurate understanding.

Think about vast amounts of time or space – billions of years or a million light years away – that have no analogy in the human earthly experience. Our intuitions are of little help here. Consider how people come to terms with huge numbers of people being killed. As Stalin said, "A single death is a tragedy and a million deaths are a statistic."[11] Our minds have trouble grasping and empathizing on this grand a scale. Our capacity to feel tops out, and we then can only generalize.

Scientists often suggest the idea that an elegant theory should also be a simple theory. They dream of a "Grand Unifying Theory" or a "Theory of Everything," by which everything can be reduced to a few basic expressions about reality. But, as we discuss later, this may be just a human preference for simple explanations. The simplicity that our minds crave may not always exist in nature. Therefore, critical thinking often requires that these preferences for commonsense explanations be challenged.

CHAPTER THREE
The Surge of Reason

Laws of Nature vs. Natural Law
"The philosophy of nature is one thing. The philosophy of value is quite another. Nothing but harm can come of confusing them."[1]
— Bertrand Russell

AN IMPORTANT DISTINCTION EMERGED as the roles of philosophy and religion were developing: This distinction divides "Laws of Nature" from the "Natural Law." The distinction between the two may seem inconsequential – especially linguistically – but the difference in meaning is important. Let's clarify these terms: Laws of nature refer to the set of immutable laws that hold the universe together. They are the same everywhere, being independent of time or location. Natural law, on the other hand, refers to the behaviors that allow humans to live in harmony with one another.

Natural law is what informs morality.

A major difference between laws of nature and natural law concerns free will. Human beings are able to violate natural law (also called moral law). For example, we can violate this law by lying and stealing. While natural law may vary slightly depending on time and location – for example in the question of whether slavery is acceptable – its trajectory is toward common understandings of justice and compassion and honesty. Natural law is like conscience: It is the "still, small voice" that is embedded in the heart of every human. The natural law is prescriptive: It tells us how to behave.

Take, for instance, the Law of Reciprocity, commonly known as the Golden Rule. Around 500 B.C., Confucius expressed this most basic moral prescription: "What you do not yourself desire, do not put before others."[2] The version from the Bible is "Do unto others as you would have them do unto you."[3] This principle is common across cultures; adhering to it, however, is not compulsory. It is a human choice.

On the other hand, laws of nature are objective and descriptive. They work to describe how reality works. Many of us have seen the bumper sticker that says, "Gravity: Not just a good idea, it is the law!" Laws of nature are not concerned with human intuitions or sacred pronouncements, and humans are unable to violate them. The French Polymath Henri Poincaré noted this when he said, "Astronomy has not only taught us that there are laws, but that from these laws there is no escape, that with them there is no possible compromise."[4]

In an article for National Public Radio, Marcelo Gleiser refers to the natural law as the laws of man: "While the laws of man seek to order and control individual and social behavior so as to make communal life less risky, the laws of Nature are deduced from long-term observation of repeatable patterns and trends."[5]

Unlike the natural law, which has subtle variances based on time and culture, the laws of nature transcend all boundaries of time, space, and culture. They are universal. We do not see a Turkish physics that is different from the physics practiced in Argentina. Nor do we see an astronomy practiced in Alabama that is different from the astronomy practiced in Australia.

Understanding that the way the universe works may be unrelated to the way that humanity works was a key realization of 17th century. It informed humanity that nature and morality were different entities that called for separate approaches and tools of understanding. Galileo succinctly summarized this view in his 1615 "Letter to Grand Duchess Christina," in which he said, "The Bible shows the way to go to heaven, not the way the heavens go."[6] (This sentiment was further developed in the 20th century, with Stephen Jay Gould's concept of "non-overlapping magisteria (NOMA)," the argument that, although science and religion both ask relevant sets of questions, they each address questions that apply to different aspects of existence.) This idea echoes separating the "is" from the "ought," a concept made famous by Scottish philosopher David Hume in the 18th century. The laws of nature are the "is," and the natural law is the "ought." Experimentalists increasingly began to view natural philosophy as the best tool with which to discover the laws of nature, and faith as the best tool with which to discover the natural law. This realization was empowering to some and threatening to others, causing people to ask new questions: Are philosophy and religion seeking different answers? Does religion lack some insights into nature? If it is lacking, is the Church qualified to speak definitively about the laws of nature? What does it imply if the laws of nature were independent of the ways that human beings live?

The Trouble with Intuition

"It is by logic one demonstrates, by intuition one invents."[7]
— Henri Poincaré

Aristotle made several extraordinary pronouncements. One famously concerned teeth, specifically the number of teeth in men and in women.[8] Aristotle said that women have fewer teeth than men. This makes intuitive sense. Women generally are smaller than men, with smaller jaws. It follows, then, that women also might have fewer teeth. Aristotle recorded this intuition accordingly. Bertrand Russell famously said, "Although he was twice married, it never occurred to him to verify this statement by examining his wives' mouths."[9]

Another famous example of the limits of intuition centers on Aristotle's pronouncement that a large, solid object falls faster than a small, solid object. This also is a sensible belief, so much so that it was "common sense" for more than almost 2000 years when Galileo circa 1590 famously dropped two different-sized steel balls from atop the tower at Pisa, thus demonstrating that objects of differing masses fall at the same rate. This was confirmed again in 1971 by Apollo 15 Comdr. David Scott who, while standing on the lunar surface, dropped a feather and a hammer simultaneously. Since the moon has no atmosphere, and therefore there was no atmospheric resistance, the two objects fell to the ground at the same rate.

Galileo advised that we use our senses with the appropriate amount of skepticism: "Where the senses fail us, reason must step in."[10] Today, we have difficulty even imagining relying solely on our intuitions and unaided sense data for understanding. An optical illusion is an example that allows us to experience the deceptive power of our raw intuitions. Vertigo is another example. Look, for instance, at the round Earth theory: Although much of our sense data tells us that the world is flat, we have to occasionally override our sense data and our intuitions with independent, objective measurements that come from tools that correct the false perceptions that our senses might provide.

Before about 500 years ago, intuition was the starting point for understanding the natural world, but it also often was the ending point. Data from direct experience rarely made its way into the process. This prejudice toward our intuitions is partly why some scientific theories such as evolution are resisted today. Earlier, we said that human beings have difficulty conceiving of huge amounts of time and space. Our senses are tuned to deal with times and distances that make sense in our lives: hours and years, feet and miles. The concept of billions of light-years just feels wrong on an intuitive level, especially when the concept of billions of light-years might challenge our religious beliefs and other sensibilities. But deep-time measurements are fruitful in our understanding of nature. Our intuitions can hold us back from understanding, so we hold them in check in favor of observational data.

Something New Under the Sun: How Facts Enabled Science

"Facts and Science are made for each other."[11]
— David Wootton

"You may force me to say what you wish; you may revile me for saying what I do. But it moves."[12]
– Galileo Galilei

While facts themselves are not new per se, they have become fundamentally influential in recent centuries. Although the concept of experiential evidence and the pushback on authority can both be dated back to the ancient Greeks, the word "fact" did not enter the English language until the late 1500s. Before then, facts were not really a thing. Science historian David Wootton shares how facts changed forever how humans obtained truth:

> If you are playing 'Rock, Paper, Scissors' you can

never be sure of who will win. Intellectual life was a bit like that when the fact was invented – some thought reason should win; some authority (particularly where questions of faith were concerned); and still others wanted to rely on experience or experiment. But when facts entered the game everything changed because there is no arguing with the facts: they always win.[13]

Prior to this increased use of facts, ancient authorities such as Aristotle and ecclesiastics were the de facto keepers of knowledge. "Data" did not have the influence that authority enjoyed. Because observational data were available to anyone through the appropriate measuring tools, authority began to become suspect where it was inconsistent with facts. Facts took on the most prestigious position on the path to truth because, as Aldous Huxley said, "facts do not cease to exist because they are ignored."[14] Facts are stubborn things that did not go away, even with resistance from authority.

The transition to prioritizing facts did not come quickly or naturally. In 1543, astronomer Nicolas Copernicus published his theory – backed by limited observational and mathematical data – arguing for heliocentrism: The sun did not orbit Earth; rather, Earth orbited the sun. Concerned with offending Church authorities, Copernicus waited until the end of his life to publish this important work. (Some say Copernicus first saw the published copy of his work on the day he died.)

There are more cautionary examples of people

openly contradicting Church authority: Logician and Protestant convert Peter Ramus openly challenged the idea that Earth was the center of the universe, as well as several other Aristotelian doctrines. In 1572, Ramus was caught up in the St. Bartholomew's Day massacre, where he was stabbed by a mob, and his body mutilated and then tossed out his window.

Later, in 1615, Galileo published his observations in support of the Copernican model. His view was backed by more-precise observational data made possible by the telescope. In spite of Galileo's popularity, his support for Copernicus' heliocentric theory put him at odds with the Church for the rest of his life.

Today, there are many ways through which we might come to believe that something is true: experience; custom; authorities such as parents, clerics or scientists; our passions; and our emotions. But facts have set the standard: "You can't argue with the facts," we say. "Just the facts, Ma'am," we say. Facts are the building blocks we use to establish common ground. They are the starting points of inquiry. We can never get to the "why" or agree on a call to action without first agreeing on the "what." The "what" currently is specific observational facts.

Faith and Reason

"God does not expect us to submit our faith to him without reason, but the very limits of our reason make faith a necessity."
— Saint Augustine

Is there anything that we could not believe on the

basis of faith?

"You can believe something really hard, and still be wrong,"[15] said Faith, a character from Jody Picoult's book "Keeping the Faith."

The relationship between faith and reason remains an area of contention to this day. The 17th-century poet John Donne wrote, "Reason is our soul's left hand. Faith her right. By these we reach divinity."[16] Scientist Francis Collins said reason and faith are complementary partners in understanding. Collins said, "Faith is not the opposite of reason. Faith rests squarely upon reason, but with the added component of revelation."[17]

This group sees faith as the foundation of reason, reserved for fundamental questions about meaning, and not simply for questions that seek to understand the natural universe. In this capacity, faith is not a tool of discovery as much as it is a tool of context, of applying metaphysical beliefs to the natural world. Proponents of faith say faith is a sacred, personal communication with the divine – a special kind of knowledge.

Critics dismiss faith as little more of an exercise in motivated reasoning. In matters concerning the physical world, we apply reason only until it contradicts our already-accepted dogmas, in which case we fall back on faith and dismiss reason as flawed. Or, as skeptic and author Michael Shermer writes, we "apply reason as far as it will go, then take the leap of faith."[18]

Critics also say that faith is an accident of birth, illustrative of how people prefer their own beliefs and those of their in-group over the beliefs of outsiders. Faith is the glue that keeps people devoted – or enslaved, depending on whom you ask – to their traditions. Faith is what keeps a Jew a Jew, a Catholic a Catholic, and a Muslim a Muslim.

This does not mean that faith has become an invalid path to truth. What changed was that the role of faith was being reexamined. Faith was becoming recognized by experimentalists as better suited not as a method of discovering information about the physical world, but as a tool for gaining spiritual transcendence.

We will not settle these views here, but obviously faith has been a source of belief that is rife for political opportunism. In the first century, Seneca the Younger observed: "Religion (faith) is regarded by the common people as true, by the wise as false, and by rulers as useful."[19] Whatever else it is, faith is a tool of power.

Reason vs Passion

"People mistakenly assume that their thinking is done by their head; it is actually done by the heart which first dictates the conclusion, then commands the head to provide the reasoning that will defend it."[20]
— Anthony de Mello

Do we love our arguments because they are good arguments, or do we love them simply because they disguise our passions so well? Do we ornament our passion-driven beliefs with strategic arguments, much the same way we decorate a Christmas tree? Where does reason fit into the process human beings use to interpret the world? This discussion is central in the modern age.

Social psychologist Jonathan Haidt wrote in his book "The Righteous Mind" that our emotional assessment comes first, and then our "inner lawyer" defends these intuitions with reasonable after-the-fact justifications and rationalizations. Haidt characterizes these two opposing yet intertwined senses as an elephant (i.e., emotion and intuition) and its rider (i.e., reason). The job of the rider is to manage the elephant, which is the stronger of the two senses. Our reason serves our passions, which come first in our process of developing a belief.

Baruch Spinoza warned us that "when a man is prey to his emotions, he is not his own master."[21] Spinoza warned we cannot hope to defeat an emotion, but only to overcome it with a stronger emotion. This applies in science, too. Science philosopher Karl Popper acknowledged, there is no such thing as "pure, disinterested, theory-free observation."[22]

Ultimately, reason and passion are doing a dance, but which one is leading can be hard to tell. Passion inspires and reason justifies. Passion intuits and reason proves.

Good Faith

"The book of nature which we have to read is written by the finger of God."[23]
— Michael Faraday

It is easy to dismiss these scientific adventurers as troublemakers who were spoiling for a fight and courting confrontation. But that would be incorrect.

These natural philosophers primarily were men of faith, people with affiliations to – and often affections for – the Church. They were looking for a path where their discoveries could coexist among accepted Church doctrines.

Copernicus himself was a member of the clergy. Giordano Bruno was a Dominican friar. Galileo and Charles Darwin both considered Church vocations. Isaac Newton was a devout believer who wrote more about religion than he wrote about physics. Johannes Kepler wrote, "I had the intention of becoming a theologian. ...but now I see how God is, by my endeavors, also glorified in astronomy, for 'the heavens declare the glory of God.'"[24] The father of modern genetics, Gregor Johan Mendel, was an Augustinian friar, and paleontologist Pierre Teilhard de Chardin spent his adult life as a Jesuit priest. These were men who believed that the understanding of God was to be found not only through revealed Scripture, but by a careful study of God's creation. "Measure what can be measured, and make measurable what cannot be measured,"[25] Galileo advised truth-seekers.

However, power is not relinquished so easily, and these new observations were largely interpreted as an encroachment on the authority of Church ecclesiastics to speak authoritatively about the natural world. Also, let's not forget that observation and experiment were new paths to finding truth. As such they posed a serious – even existential – threat to the body of knowledge that already existed.

Later in the 17th century, Spinoza was critical of the Calvinist Church for speaking authoritatively on matters of the natural world, and for trying to control the speech of others: "What can be more calamitous than that men should be regarded as enemies and put to death, not for any crime or misdeed, but for being of independent mind?"[26] Will Durant said, "Woe to him who teaches men faster than they can learn,"[27] It was not until 1992 that the Catholic Church formally acknowledged that Galileo was correct in his belief that Earth moves around the sun.

CHAPTER FOUR
Science

A New System

"Human understanding is like a false mirror, which, receiving rays irregularly, distorts and discolors the nature of things by mingling its own nature with it."[1]
— Francis Bacon

IN 1620, POLITICIAN AND experimentalist Francis Bacon published "Novum Organum," an ambitious response to Aristotle's ancient work about logic, "The Organon."

Bacon argued that the past body of human knowledge had been infected by traditional dogmas and superstition, authority and intuition. He argued that humanity needed to start from scratch, building a new body of knowledge based on careful and systematic observation and a slow but stable collection of observations stripped of views that were rooted in authority and tradition.

This plan was ambitious, and it revolutionized learning. The frontispiece to "Novum Organum" showed a historical metaphor: an illustration of a galleon setting sail from a familiar but corrupted port and into a broad, uncharted sea of knowledge and understanding.

"Novum Organum" contains some of the finest prose of the era. In the preface (from which the quotations that follow are taken), Bacon sets out his argument that knowledge has been harmed by people who have wasted their time merely curating past information, as if nature were "a thing already searched out and understood." This arrogant assumption that nature was already a known quantity had been successful only in "quenching and stopping inquiry." It carried with it a "presumption of pronouncing on everything"; its adherents were "impatient horses champing the bit." The result was that society did not possess real certainty about anything.

Therefore, Bacon continued, human efforts to understand must start again with the assumption that "absolutely nothing can be known" from these past efforts. Studies of natural philosophy must reorganize to become systematically experimental and skeptical, arriving at truths "not by arguing, but by trying." The goal was not a single reveal of truth but, instead, "progressive stages of certainty." The truth was not a finite destination but a process of discovery. His book (the title of which means "New Organ") presented "a new and certain path for the mind to proceed." Bacon said that it would strive to remove centuries of intellectual sediment brought about by the "daily intercourse and conversation of life, occupied with unsound doctrines and beset on all sides by vain imaginations."

At that time in history, logic had come "too late to the rescue," and had canonized spurious information from past authorities and traditions, "fixing errors rather than disclosing truth." Bacon presented a process with which to rein in intuition, where the mind will not be allowed simply to "take its own course," but rather will be "guided at every step; and the business be done as if by machinery."

In this system, Bacon supplemented intuition with measurement, resolving the "truth" equation as "truth = intuition + reason + data." "Seek not pretty and probable conjectures," he said, "but certain and demonstrable knowledge." Bacon named two elements that echo our categories of intuition and experimentation: "Anticipation of the Mind" and "Interpretation of Nature." He prescribed a reset, a "great restoration of learning and knowledge" that anticipated Descartes' famous 1637 statement, "I think, therefore I am."

Finally, Bacon presented his famous "Idols of the Mind," the four impediments to gathering knowledge. First are the "Idols of the Tribe," our human-centric tendency to assume that reality is best described from a human perspective. Second are the "Idols of the Cave," which refer to the individual prejudices and filters from which we approach any phenomena. Third are the "Idols of the Marketplace," which are the limitations that we find while communicating through the imprecisions of language. Finally, are the "Idols of the Theater," which are the groups of subconscious cultural prejudices that today make up the "intrinsic bias."

Bacon's Novum Organum often is cited as the cornerstone of the scientific revolution. After it, the modern world would change fundamentally and permanently. This change was not limited to science. This new scientific outlook affects all human efforts to form beliefs. Scientific discovery and building robust beliefs largely use the same methods.

Science

"It is not what the man of science believes that distinguishes him, but how and why he believes it. His beliefs are tentative, not dogmatic; they are based on evidence, not on authority or intuition."[2]
— Bertrand Russell

"No Science, No Twitter."
— Words on popular T-shirts today

Nothing defines our age as completely as science. Nothing even comes close, and the main reason for this is obvious: Science works. Think of how much we work using a collection of electronic devices – made possible by science – that allow us to easily communicate around the globe. We travel across the land, over the seas and through the air with the most amazing sense of unamazement. We live two or three times as long as our ancestors thanks to the advancements of medicine brought about by science.

The approximately 100-year span of the Scientific Revolution saw a great reorganization of how humans establish belief. This period was significant in the way reasoning developed. Let's note how replete was this period with founding figures of science.

As discussed earlier here, many scholars credit Francis Bacon (1561-1626) with being the first "modern" man and the founder of the scientific method. Baruch Spinoza (1632-1677) and René Descartes (1596-1650) are both cited as founders of modern philosophy. This period witnessed an unprecedented flowering of discovery based on observation. Galileo Galilei (1564-1642) published his most noteworthy findings in the first decade of the 17th century. In 1660, chemist Robert Boyle (1627-1691) dropped a feather and a coin inside his newly invented vacuum pump (in which air resistance had been removed), thus confirming Galileo's famous demonstration at the Tower of Pisa that objects fall at a constant rate. Also active in this period were astronomer Johannes Kepler (1571-1630), famous for his observations about planetary motion; and the developers of the microscope, Anton van Leeuwenhoek (1632-1723) and Robert Hooke (1635-1703). William Harvey (1578-1657) performed his landmark work on anatomy. The year that Galileo died welcomed the birth of mathematician and physicist Isaac Newton (1642-1726).

What was becoming the modern world saw the emergence of a new way of knowing. Rigorous and reliable, it was also independently verifiable and universal. Twentieth-century astronomer Neil deGrasse Tyson boasted, "The good thing about science is that it's true whether or not you believe in it."³ Such a boast is justified with the ubiquity and influence of science in modern life. Science is so fundamental in our daily lives that we hardly even notice. Even people who organize their lives around other principles such as religion largely fall back on science when they seek medical knowledge, food security, entertainment and communication. Science has become the backdrop of our lives, the proverbial "water in which we swim."

Science is a Process

"Science is not a body of knowledge nor a system of belief; it is just a term which describes humankind's incremental acquisition of understanding through observation."[4]
— Tim Minchin

Science is not a destination; it is a process. It is not the address of truth, but simply a reliable vehicle in which to carry us there. Science provides the best way that we know for discovering truths. For the scientist, truth is to be found through the careful application of our reason, where we incrementally and consistently improve our understanding.

The basic scientific process involves proposing a question, gathering data about that question, hypothesizing and testing that hypothesis. Then repeating the process. Similar processes drive all kinds of rigorous learning. Unlike with our senses and our emotions, where we have no choice but to view the world through these filters, following the scientific process is mostly optional. Still, the scientific process is similar to the iterative process of "hunch-test-repeat" thinking that all human beings use to one degree or another.

We all are born with the potential for rationality, and generally we consider ourselves as rational. But actually, using our rationality by developing our reasoning skills is more comparable to playing the guitar – we do not have to do it, and if we choose to do it, we don't have to do it well. Most people who do not practice or develop the skill of playing the guitar do not also claim to know how to play the guitar. However, we think that being reasonable is more comparable to driving: Just as the average driver believes they are an above-average driver, the average thinker believes they are an above-average thinker.

When we hear someone say that they "believe in science," what do they mean? Is this a politically correct statement that they commit to certain beliefs about reality that are in vogue, such as belief in climate change or in the theory of evolution, or is this a statement defined by a process of following the evidence? If the scientific consensus comes out against evolution, for example, a follower of science will choose data over consistency every time. They update their beliefs according to the most recent data.

People use this process – questioning, gathering data, hypothesizing and testing that hypothesis – inconsistently and incompletely. We use science only up to a point, after which we cut to a conclusion that we arrive at via one of the other paths to understanding, such as authority or tradition. In the resulting ambiguity, not only do people not agree on the answers, they often do not agree even on the questions that need be asked.

This partial commitment to the reasoning process is why there is so little consensus on many matters. As Bertrand Russell observed, "most controversies are about those matters as to which there is no good evidence either way."[5] When people run up against a lack of data, instead of simply holding back from coming to a conclusion, they abandon the reasoning process altogether, or they contaminate it with biases or a blind deference to authority or an appeal to the supernatural. The correct use of the scientific process brings about consensus. Therefore, the wise scientist sticks to the process, and avoids coming to a conclusion prematurely. They withhold judgment until the data warrants one. Their commitment is to the process, not to the belief.

Scientific Skepticism

"At the heart of science is an essential balance between two seemingly contradictory attitudes – an openness to new ideas, no matter how bizarre or counterintuitive they may be, and the most ruthless skeptical scrutiny of all ideas, old and new. This is how deep truths are winnowed from deep nonsense."[6]
— Carl Sagan

Science works largely due to an "institutionalized doubt" built into the scientific process. We explore this key ingredient to doing effective science (and any critical thinking) from several directions over the next sections of this chapter. Through doubt we encourage skepticism and the quick acknowledgement – and correction – of errors.

Implied in many religions is that, at some previous point, at least with certain individuals, or in certain circumstances, people transcended nature into a metaphysical reality. They witnessed things fully and reported them accurately to people who recorded them in their entirety so people could pass them down through the ages faithfully. The challenge for religion, therefore, is to preserve and even return to this past state. Often, this is done through proverbs, divine commandments and revelations.

The methods of science could not be more different. Scientific truths are discovered, not recovered. Scientists approach truth by persistently and incrementally moving forward. Science assumes that human knowledge will always be incomplete, and that is OK. Science does not suggest a specific remedy to this slow advancement. It simply accepts that advancements toward truth happen slowly: "Truth is called the daughter of time, not of authority,"[7] said Francis Bacon.

The essence of this path forward is scientific skepticism. "Skepticism, like chastity, should not be relinquished too readily,"[8] said philosopher George Santayana. Science tells us that what was accepted as true in the past may have actually been only a partial truth, or even an error entirely. Therefore, we must test and revisit these beliefs over time so they develop a certain consistency. In science, a long string of failed experiments means that we are that much closer to a truth. When we fail repeatedly to disprove a theory, only then does that theory become a "working" truth.

Science and the Admission of Ignorance

"The plague of man is boasting of his knowledge."[9]
— Michel de Montaigne

Perhaps the most spectacular attribute of science – and also its least understood attribute – is its reversal of that most human of traits: the prejudice that leads us to assume that we are correct. Authors Steven Shapin and Simon Shaffer refer to this predilection for humans to assume the correctness of their community as an "unreflective membership." In their book, "The Miniature Guide to the Art of Asking Essential Questions," authors Richard Paul and Linda Elder writes:

> Through self-deception, humans live with the unrealistic but confident sense that we have fundamentally figured out the way things actually are, and that we have done this objectively. We naturally believe in our intuitive perceptions – however inaccurate. In other words, though human thinking is often flawed, it nevertheless sees itself as right, correct, in possession of 'the truth.'[10]

Scientific theories reverse this prejudice, making the assumption that we are not correct. Galileo said that "to be humane, we must ever be ready to pronounce that wise, ingenious and modest statement 'I do not know.'"[11] Therefore, a central question a scientist asks is not, "How do I know that I am right?" but, rather, "How can I find out that I am wrong?" Yuval Noah

Harari said: "The Scientific Revolution has not been a revolution of knowledge. It has been above all a revolution of ignorance. The great discovery that launched the Scientific Revolution was the discovery that humans do not know the answers to their most important questions."[12] In science, certainty is rare and skepticism is common. Harari writes that modern science is unique in that it "openly admits collective ignorance regarding the most important questions."

When you shake a water bottle that is either completely full or completely empty, you do not hear anything. But when the bottle is partly full, shaking it makes some noise. Substitute water for knowledge, and the point is clear: A little knowledge is noisy and arrogant. A lot of knowledge is quiet and does not boast. "Our knowledge can only be finite," said science philosopher Karl Popper, "while our ignorance must necessarily be infinite."[13] It is "when men are most sure and arrogant they are commonly most mistaken,"[14] warned David Hume.

Intellectual humility – or epistemological modesty – is a prerequisite for effective examination, specifically in scientific inquiry. This is the scientific equivalent of the Zen "beginner's mind." "To know what you know and what you do not know, that is true knowledge," said Confucius. Science always starts with an assessment of our level of ignorance.

Scientific Truth is Provisional Only
"We must operate with partial knowledge, and be provisionally content with probabilities."[15]

— Ariel Durant

Implied in scientific inquiry is the idea that inquiry is never complete.

Scientific truth is based only on likelihoods that, as in the case with the theory of gravity, may reach a high degree of certitude. But they nevertheless remain, in principle at least, incomplete. Scientific truth is true only until it is not true. That is, it is true until a more complete explanation comes along. Scientific inquiry is the original "growth mindset." It assumes that it is incomplete, and open to correction and new information. Science gets better at getting better, constantly improving itself. But although science aims in the direction of truth, it does not expect to find it and would never canonize it.

As a result, the scientific vocabulary uses words such as "tentative," "probable" and "likelihood."

Science is Self-Correcting

"There are many hypotheses in science which are wrong. That's perfectly all right; they're the aperture to finding out what's right. Science is a self-correcting process. To be accepted, new ideas must survive the most rigorous standards of evidence and scrutiny."[16]
— Carl Sagan

The scientific vocabulary also includes words such as "cumulative," "additive" and "iterative." Because scientific truths are provisional only, errors are not only implied, they are expected and even welcomed. "Scientific ideas, like evolution itself, may change dramatically over time, but they do so by the accumulation of small transformations and differing interpretations,"[17] Naomi Oreskes writes in "Why Trust Science?"

Science is optimized to identify and purge its errors quickly. It rigorously identifies, corrects and learns from its mistakes, which sets science apart from many tradition-based ways of knowing. "What only science can promise. ...is a continuous, midcourse self-correction, as additional experimental and observational evidence accumulates,"[18] said Mario Livio.

Science is consistent in method, but not in content. The goal of science is not to prove, but to understand. In fact, scientists make a name for themselves by growing the knowledge base, by demonstrating places where the current model falls short and how they can improve upon it. Newton expressed this well when he famously said, "If I have seen further it is by standing on the shoulders of giants." Harari contrasts the paths of the experimentalist Darwin and the prophet Muhammad:

> Muhammad himself very quickly began to argue that *he* knew the full truth, and his followers began calling him 'the Seal of Prophets'. Henceforth, there was no need for revelations beyond those given to Muhammad. ...[however,] Darwin never argued that he was 'the Seal of Biologists,' and that he had solved the riddle of life once and for all. After centuries of extensive scientific research, scientists admit that they still don't have any good explanation of how our brains produce consciousness. Physicists admit they

do not know what caused the Big Bang, or how to reconcile quantum mechanics with relativity.[19]

Scientists respect contributions from past traditions and scientists. But they do not – in principal at least – sanctify them.

Do Not Fool Yourself

"The first principle is that you must not fool yourself – and you are the easiest person to fool. So you have to be very careful about that. After you've not fooled yourself, it's easy not to fool other scientists."[20]
— Richard Feynman

People mostly believe what they want to believe. It is the natural state of humanity to assume that our beliefs are the correct ones and then to buttress them with whatever evidence and arguments we can find. This tendency does not mean that our beliefs necessarily are incorrect, but should remind us that our natural state is to favor our own views over the views of others, and to assume that our beliefs probably are the correct ones. It is an easy step for humans to go through life casually proving their correctness while failing to pay attention to contrary evidence.

The scientific process is designed to counter this tendency, also. "The real purpose of the scientific method is to make sure nature hasn't misled you into thinking you know something you actually don't know,"[21] warned Robert Pirsig, author of "Zen and the Art of Motorcycle Maintenance." The scientific method is a guardrail to help us not fall for what is the most common of human traps, where we accept a belief simply because it is appealing.

Destroy the Falsehood

"To kill an error is as good a service as, and sometimes even better than, the establishing of a new truth or fact."[22]
— Charles Darwin

In today's science-driven world, young scientists distinguish themselves not by defending and upholding the work of past scientists. Instead, they aim at advancing knowledge through destroying the existing paradigm. They establish what journalist Carl Bernstein refers to as "the best attainable version of the truth." This best version is attained not in a spirit of aggression or demolition, but in a spirit of learning and truth-seeking.

In science, as in all understanding, progress toward success often is made by failing. Thomas Huxley said, "The attainment of scientific truth has been effected, to a great extent, by the help of scientific errors."[23] Further, keeping the scientific floor swept clear of bad ideas is essential to the discovery of good ideas. The best way to certainty is to establish falsities. Writer P.C. Hodgell wrote, "That which can be destroyed by the truth should be."[24] In fact, destroying a falsehood has a more lasting impact; like removing a stone from the path, removing the falsehood improves the path.

Science is public

"Science does not conceal its evidence or rest its case on mysteries or private revelations, but makes everything public, so that all experts, and even the serious layman, can examine and weigh the claims and arguments of scientists to an extent not possible in any other field, creating the most effective check against individual bias that humans can devise."[25]
— Richard Carrier

Science is the original "open source" activity. Any set of scientific facts is, in principle, accessible to anyone, and people from anywhere are able to participate in a shared and transparent scientific quest. While there are centers of scientific expertise – and even areas of secrecy such as defense – no particular place calls itself the home of science. There is no Vatican, Mecca or Holy Land of science.

CHAPTER FIVE
A Good Theory

What is a Theory?

"Creationists make it sound as though a 'theory' is something you dreamt up after being drunk all night."[1]
— Isaac Asimov

LEE MCINTYRE, IN HIS book "The Scientific Attitude: Defending Science from Denial, Fraud, and Pseudoscience," explains the false conception that science arrives at either permanent truths or complete falsehoods. Of critics of science he said:

> [They often] seem to reflect the idea that science is all or nothing: that we can either be 100 percent certain that our theory has been verified by the evidence, or we are completely at sea because – until the definitive experiment has been done – one theory is as good as any else.[2]

For purposes of this book, we will define a theory broadly, as simply an explanation.

Let's say I encounter a phenomenon while I am driving my car down the highway. Let's say it's a strange noise. This is the observational beginning: I hear a noise.

Hunches and assumptions flood my mind: Where is the noise coming from? Is it a rhythmic sound? Will slowing down change anything about the noise? How about speeding up? Turning? What will happen if I open the window? Will that help me hear the noise more clearly?

Some of these intuitions are testable, and we call these hypotheses. I can slow down. I can speed up. I can turn. I can roll the window down. A hypothesis is a single, testable effort toward an explanation.

As I begin to work these hypotheses, some of them test true. For instance, rolling down the window helps me hear the noise more clearly (now I can tell that it is emanating from the back of the car). Some of these hypotheses test false. For instance, turning does not seem to change the noise.

I collect these hypotheses into a bundle, and now I have the beginnings of a theory.

A Good Theory is Explanatory

"I would rather have questions that can't be answered than answers that can't be questioned."[3]
— Richard P. Feynman

In 1687, England's "greatest scientist," Sir Isaac

Newton, published his "Philosophiae Naturalis Principia Mathematica" (Mathematical Principles of Natural Philosophy), in which he explained the workings of the known universe. The subjects of "The Principia," as the book has come to be called, include discussions of gravity, motion and planetary orbits. It is often cited as the most important science book in history. For hundreds of years, it contained the best explanations of the laws of nature available.

My noise-from-my-car theory doesn't do much at this point. In fact, it is little more than a few hunches and tested hypotheses. But that is OK. Karl Popper said, "a theory that explains everything, explains nothing." We need to stay targeted. Even at this embryonic stage, my theory is able to suggest small explanations, such as since the noise is coming from the rear of my car, the sound is probably not being caused by the engine.

I can use this data to create more hypotheses. For instance, since my hypothesis that rolling down the window may help me hear the noise more clearly, and since testing this hypothesis revealed that the noise is emanating from the back of the car, I have the beginnings of an explanation for the noise: It is not emanating from the under the hood, so it is probably not the engine.

Theories that do not explain even this much are called theories of "explanatory impotence" – they are mostly useless. A theory does not need to explain everything (the "all" or "nothing" situation that we mentioned earlier), but it should explain some things. This is why supernatural theories often are criticized – they lack real explanations. They assume a magic answer, but magic is not an explanation.

This is the first criterion of a theory: A good theory explains something.

A Good Theory is Predictive

"A theory established with the help of twenty facts must explain thirty, and lead to the discovery of ten more."[4]
— Jean-Baptiste Dumas

In 1915, 26-year-old Albert Einstein first proposed his general theory of relativity. This theory diverged from the long-revered explanations of the physical universe set forth by Isaac Newton. As is the case with anything that challenges the current order, Einstein's theory met with resistance from those who stuck to the traditional Newtonian explanations. Also – importantly – Einstein's theory was not at this point predictive. It was an abstract theory that had never been tested directly.

Eventually, Einstein offered a prediction. A total eclipse of the sun that was to occur in 1919 offered a way to test Einstein's general theory of relativity. The theory predicted that the apparent positions of stars appearing in the line of the eclipse would shift once the light from these stars passed near the sun, because the light would be bent as it passed near the sun's gravity.

Expeditions of astronomers were sent out to different continents to observe the eclipse. The astronomers carefully measured (and photographed) the stars' positions during the eclipse, and then again after the eclipse. The results of the experiment confirmed that light passing near the sun did indeed appear to bend, and these stars appeared to change position, just as the theory had predicted. Light was bent by gravity. Einstein's theory made and survived a prediction.

Later that year, the theory was formally presented to the Royal Society, complete with a portrait of Isaac Newton overseeing the ceremony. The tests were repeated three years later, during another solar eclipse. Today, radio telescopes and other technologies have verified the theory again and again.

Richard Carrier said of a theory the following:

> So the more predictions entailed by a proposition that are fulfilled, the more reasonable it is for us to believe it. And vice versa: the more predictions a claim entails that actually fail to transpire when investigated, the less reasonable it is for us to believe it.[5]

Now back to our noise. I am developing a working theory that the noise is coming from the back of my car. Using this theory, I predict that slowing down the car will probably affect the noise. So I slow down – and sure enough, the tempo of the noise decreases. My working theory just made a successful prediction! So I continue growing the theory. Let's make another prediction: If I roll down the car window again, ease up on the gas, and the listen to the noise, I should hear the rhythmic *thwap!* sound of a flat tire.

Here we have the second component of a theory: A good theory makes predictions.

A Good Theory is Falsifiable

"Our belief in any particular natural law cannot have a safer basis than our unsuccessful critical attempts to refute it."[6]
— Karl Popper

Karl Popper championed the powerful idea that a theory must provide a way to destroy itself. That is, it must offer a way to be proven wrong. It must be falsifiable. If it provides no way that we can disprove it, we should not be surprised that the theory is never proven wrong. Popper said, "It is part of my thesis that all our knowledge grows only through the correcting of our mistakes."[7] Therefore, a good theory not only is a theory that has never been proven false but, more importantly is one that exposes itself to ways where it can be shown to be false. When Einstein proposed the eclipse experiment, he exposed the theory to the possibility of falsification. If his prediction during the eclipse had turned out to be false – that is, if the starlight did not bend – the theory would have been falsified and then abandoned. Lee McIntyre said that even when a theory survives a falsifiable experiment, the theory is still not really true on a scientific level. He said:

> Even when a theory succeeds it cannot be accepted as true – or even partially true – it must always inhabit the purgatory of having merely survived 'so far'. ... Scientific reasoning is thus forced to make peace with the fact that it will always be open ended, because the data is open ended, too.[8]

Scientific theories are never given the mantle of truth. The same principle of falsification applied to Darwin's theory of evolution. The theory that complex lifeforms evolve from less-complex lifeforms led to the prediction that more complex mammals should show up in the fossil record after less complex reptiles. So, if we found rabbit bones in the Precambrian, Darwin's theory of evolution would be falsified. But mammal bones do not appear before reptile bones in the fossil record; they come after, so the theory survives another day.

Explanation, prediction, and falsification comprise the triumvirate through which a theory cycles. This is why scientists – and anyone else interested in uncovering truth – need to be comfortable with uncertainty, and committed to following the data, wherever it goes. By showing, through falsification, the way not to go, science is showing us a way to go. Physicist Enrico Fermi said, "an experiment disproving a prediction is a discovery."[9] That is, falsification of a theory vindicates the method and moves the inquiry forward.

Back to my "flat tire" theory. I roll down the window and listen again. It sounds more like a metallic scraping noise than it does the *thwap* that a flat tire might make. Furthermore, my car is handling just fine. Hmm.

My theory that the noise is a flat tire has just been falsified. Therefore, I reject this theory, and I have to reassess the data and revise my theory to accommodate the reality that my hypotheses failed. The more ways a theory offers to disprove itself – but is not disproven –

the stronger that theory becomes. My "flat tire" theory offered up least two ways to falsify itself. First, if I do not hear a flat-tire sound when I roll down the window, the noise is probably not from a flat tire. Second, if my car is riding smoothly, the noise is probably not from a flat tire.

Here is the third essential component of a scientific theory: A scientific theory must be falsifiable.

Russell's Teapot: You Can't Prove a Negative

"You could claim that anything's real if the only basis for believing in it is that nobody's proved it doesn't exist!"[10]
— J.K. Rowling

One of the more famous examples of a non-falsifiable theory comes from 20th-century philosopher Bertrand Russell's "celestial teapot" example:

> If I were to suggest that between the Earth and Mars there is a china teapot revolving about the sun in an elliptical orbit, nobody would be able to disprove my assertion provided I were careful to add that the teapot is too small to be revealed even by our most powerful telescopes.
>
> But if I were to go on to say that, since my assertion cannot be disproved, it is an intolerable presumption on the part of human reason to doubt it, I should rightly be thought to be talking nonsense.
>
> If, however, the existence of such a teapot were affirmed in ancient books, taught as the sacred truth every Sunday, and instilled into the minds of children at school, hesitation to believe in its existence would become a mark of eccentricity and

entitle the doubter to the attentions of the psychiatrist in an enlightened age or of the Inquisitor in an earlier time.[11]

The point behind Russell's thought experiment is to show that a claim must not be accepted as true simply because it cannot be disproved. There are many variations of this experiment. There is the one that argues for the existence of the "flying spaghetti monster." Or Carl Sagan's extended theme of a dragon living in his garage – and when anyone tries to verify the existence of the dragon, the proponent adds new criteria that protect the claim from falsification. The dragon is invisible. *And* it leaves no tracks. *And* it is not the kind of dragon that spits fire. (You get the idea.)

Another way we look at this principle is through the "absence of evidence" aphorism: "The absence of evidence is not evidence of absence," or simply "You can't prove a negative."

Theories that are not falsifiable tend to persist. As we will discuss later in Chapter 6, this is why many conspiracy theories tend to stick around: Because a theory does not open itself to falsification, many will incorrectly interpret this inability for the theory to be proven false as proof that the theory is true. Meager plausibility becomes certainty.

Next, the fact that the theory has then stood the test of time is incorrectly interpreted as more evidence that the theory is true: "Because people have believed this for years, it must probably be true." But because scientific truth is always provisional and based on probabilities, we might read this aphorism as "The absence of evidence is not the always evidence of absence, but usually it is." That is, if there is no proof forthcoming, the assumption should not be that a theory is true.

Occam's Razor: Simple Answers Are Likely the Correct Answers

"Is it more probable that nature should go out of her course, or that a man should tell a lie?"[12]
— Thomas Paine

Occam's Razor, named after the 13th-century philosopher and friar William of Occam, is the law of simplicity or parsimony: It advises us that when we have two adequate explanations of the same phenomenon, we should give preference to the explanation that is more simple.

A famous example of Occam's Razor comes from the early 19th century, when French mathematician Pierre-Simon Laplace (1749–1827) presented to Napoleon a theory on the origins of the cosmos. The emperor asked Laplace where God fit into his theory. Laplace is reported to have replied plainly, "I had no need of that hypothesis."[13] Occam's Razor plays to the preference that scientists have for an elegant simplicity in nature. Laplace's explanation worked fine without an appeal to a divine being, so why add one?

Simplicity in nature has not been the scientific experience in complex theories such as the theories of relativity and quantum mechanics. Richard Carrier writes Occam's Razor today is today in preventing an intellectual overreach: "Though scientists seek the simple, nature does not always give them what they want. ...This rule is correct not because nature is simple, but because humans are ignorant. Occam's Razor aims at preventing you from claiming more than you know."[14] Sometimes understanding is not simple.

CHAPTER SIX

The Grand Conspiracy, and Others

The Grand Conspiracy

"There is a cult of ignorance in the United States, and there has always been. The strain of anti-intellectualism has been a constant thread winding its way through our political and cultural life, nurtured by the false notion that democracy means that 'my ignorance is just as good as your knowledge.'"[15]
— Isaac Asimov

A CONSPIRACY IS A coordinated effort by two or more people to do something nefarious – something illegal, treacherous or surreptitious. The Lincoln assassination was the result of a conspiracy, as was the 9/11 attack. Conspiracies can and do happen. In fact, basically two or more people who coordinate in a nefarious activity constitute a conspiracy.

A "grand conspiracy" assumes a conspiracy not of

just a few people, but entire segments of society: political groups and institutions, ethnic groups, religious groups, socioeconomic groups. Examples of current alleged grand conspiracies include the government effort in Roswell, N.M., to keep secret a recovered alien spaceship and alien remains. Another is the alleged conspiracy to cover up a government-planned assassination of President John F. Kennedy. More recent examples include the "plandemic": the alleged orchestrated effort by nefarious agents to seize control of the world economy by shutting it down, using COVID-19 as a pretext, and the alleged Democrat/mass media conspiracy to steal the 2020 presidential election.

A grand conspiracy is a master conspiracy that leverages all sorts of human cognitive vulnerabilities. According to Stephen Novella, in his video series "Your Deceptive Mind: A Scientific Guide to Critical Thinking," grand conspiracies are "built on cognitive biases and maintained with logical fallacies."[16] Then they are "further fueled by errors in perception and memory."[17] A grand conspiracy is sort of a "super spreader" of bad thought, taking over a person's ability to think critically and leaving its victims epistemologically crippled.

Grand conspiracies usually concern the nefarious and the secretive. They exist in opposition to an accepted, mainstream narrative or explanation of an event. Grand conspiracy theorists – let's call them GCTs – distrust specific authorities and data. They also refuse to accept the burden of proof, demanding that their critics either refute or accept their unproven claims.

They also expand the conspiracy as needed in order to ensure their existence. The wider the conspiracy, the more difficult it is to prove, but perhaps that is acceptable when conspiracy theorists refuse to accept the burden of proof, anyway: "THEY must be in on it, too!"

Grand conspiracies are especially dangerous because they discourage their followers from testing their claims systematically against reality. A grand conspiracy eventually becomes a closed belief system, immune to refutation. Believers in the grand conspiracy become highly resistant to counter-evidence. As is the case with a bad scientific theory, the grand conspiracy persists not because it is proven true, but because it cannot be proven false. They exist on the edges of reason, even to the point that instances of evidence that contradicts the conspiracy is interpreted as proof of the conspiracy. Think of cult behavior, where most sound arguments critical of the cult are interpreted merely as a fulfillment that the group will be persecuted.

Grand conspiracies are distrustful of authority and are suspicious of expertise or specialization. Robert Green Ingersoll said, "It is what people do not know that they persecute each other about."[18] A passionate and ill-informed suspicion increases in proportion to the ignorance that surrounds a subject, and it is "not a simple lack of knowledge," as Karl Popper said, "but an active aversion to knowledge, the refusal to know, issuing from cowardice, pride, or laziness of mind."[19] A grand conspiracy sanctifies ignorance in order to preserve its own existence.

A grand conspiracy consists of three main groups:

the conspirators, the masses of people who are unwitting dupes of the conspiracy and the GCTs who are the few who have successfully connected the dots and uncovered the conspiracy. The GCTs then constitute a special "army of resistance" against the conspiracy. Grand conspiracies are harmful in that they cast doubt over institutions and over the loyalty of those who disbelieve the conspiracy. (Ironically, unreasoned doubt can look a lot like reasoned skepticism. Conspiracies can even sometimes have a positive influence in an open society because they demand transparency and accountability.)

In this chapter, we will look into various cognitive traps, which are the patterns of poor thinking to which humans are susceptible. We will also look at logical fallacies, which are errors in logic, from the perspective of a grand conspiracy.

Confirmation Bias

"Nothing is so firmly believed as that which we least know."[20]
— Michel de Montaigne

Confirmation bias is the process that prompts people to overvalue data that confirm their assumptions and to undervalue data that question these assumptions. Francis Bacon described confirmation bias as the root of superstition, saying that it is the tendency that "men observe when things hit, and not when they miss; and commit to memory the one, and forget and pass over the other."[21] The natural state of humans, remember, is not rationality, but self-interest. We tend to select evidence based on its ability to justify our beliefs. Often, reason requires that we override this behavior.

Confirmation bias leads us to construct a reality that reinforces our beliefs and prejudices. Essentially, any belief system – from politics to religion to our own moral behaviors – looks better the more that we disregard any contrary information. GCTs are particularly prone to confirmation bias; they assume the veracity of their beliefs, just as they assume that any contrary narratives are false. This bias can be especially damaging when combined with what is called the "Ostrich Effect," whereby people do not just demote data contrary to their views, but actually ignore it altogether, preventing any shared reality to be built. The conspiracy theory becomes the filter through which they view the world. To an extent, we all do this. Therefore, we all need to take special care to be receptive to considering information that is contrary to our beliefs.

Attacking the Person

"When the debate is lost, slander becomes the tool of the loser."[22]
— Attributed to Socrates

The Ad Hominem Fallacy is often the first logical fallacy of which people become aware. It is also probably the most common fallacy, especially in today's online environment.

Road rage gives rise to an emotional state that often leads to the ad hominem attack. People feel insulated in the perceived anonymity of their automobiles and therefore indulge in a level of aggressiveness toward a stranger that they would never exhibit in face-to-face situations.

This tendency to dehumanize has only worsened in the online age, when people feel even more shielded in their homes, behind their computer screen, fingers poised and full of keyboard-fueled courage. Civility (like clothing) is not required online, since online communication is usually a text-only activity. Non-textual forms of communication – such as facial expressions, body language and tone – are missing from the message, as are the courtesies of small talk and other efforts to connect, understand and communicate empathy. These characteristics of respectful discussion are replaced by insults driven by the "the best defense is a good offense" strategy: Attack before you are attacked. Author Criss Jami said insults often replace good arguments: "Since many of us are. ... lacking in good arguments, we are then prone to being well-versed in insults."[23]

The combination of bad argumentation and online anonymity makes the internet a poor and potentially destructive environment for discussion. We too easily forget that the object of our rage is human – just like ourselves. We deride their character, question their motives, assume their allegiances, attack their reasoning and mock their gullibility. Only rarely do we respond to their arguments.

Because a grand conspiracy thrives on division, disparaging the motives of people is its core strategy. Scroll through the comments on a YouTube video about any controversial subject and see how quickly comments turn into insults and even become hateful. Ad hominem attacks are a serious threat to a society in which participating in civil discussion, finding unity and showing goodwill is essential.

This vilification of an opponent is sometimes called the "fundamental attribution error," which is the belief that people who don't share our views are not just misguided, but actually are following an intentionally malevolent agenda. For example, one of the five core beliefs of the QAnan grand conspiracy, according to an opinion piece by CNN.com's Aaron Weaver, is that the Democratic Party is not just in error, but actually is a sinister and hostile enemy force.[24] Rather than displaying good will perhaps by asking the opponent a friendly question in order to establish common ground, the GCT often just responds with an insult, closing down all hope of respectful discussion. Instead of a simple goodwill effort to understand, the exchange becomes a battle between light and dark forces.

Application vs Implication: The Appeal to Consequences fallacy

"It is difficult to get a man to understand something, when his salary depends on his not understanding it."[25]
— Upton Sinclair

The Appeal to Consequences Fallacy is the tendency for people to construct their beliefs – not on the basis of evidence and good reasons – but rather based on their comfort with the implications of the belief. Consider the person who is addicted to smoking cigarettes and rejects the belief that cigarette smoking causes cancer because such a belief would present a challenge to his addiction. Or consider the person who fears that believing in evolution might lead to a harsh and destructive "survival of the fittest" attitude in society, and therefore rejects this theory.

We should not reject a belief based on our distaste for the consequences that having such a belief might bring. Instead, we do our best to believe dispassionately and according to evidence, and not because of our like or dislike of the implications of a particular belief.

Consider the geocentrism vs. heliocentrism controversy from the early 17th century. The resistance to the heliocentric theory was not the result of a growing body of data showing that the sun and the planets orbit Earth. In fact, the data were increasingly showing that Earth and the planets orbited the sun. However, the belief was rejected by the Church not because of data but because of negative implications that this theory might have on religious doctrine.

Regarding climate change, if Earth heats up even a few degrees, the consequences will probably be catastrophic. If the measures required to address climate change seem prohibitively disruptive, we should not reject the belief that climate change poses a problem. Instead, we should continue to acknowledge the problem, but possibly reject the solution as too costly. Let's ask: Do the costs of stopping climate change using this solution outweigh the benefits? The argument then progresses systematically from whether the belief is true to whether the solution is workable and finally to whether the benefits of solving the problem outweigh the costs of the solution. Those who reject the existence of a problem simply because they do not like the solution are interrupting the reasoning process altogether.

The Appeal to Consequences Fallacy also works the other way. Just as we should not reject a belief because we do not like the implications of the belief, we should not accept a belief simply because we like what this belief implies for us. For example, we should not be a believer in the superiority of the male gender simply because nature has made us male. In this case, the Appeal to Consequences Fallacy leads to "motivated reasoning," which we discuss next.

I Want to Believe - Motivated Reasoning

"Those who fear the facts will forever try to discredit the fact-finders."[26]
— Denis Diderot

Motivated reasoning is the sibling of confirmation bias. While confirmation bias encourages us to give preference to data that supports our preferred conclusion, motivated reasoning comes into play even before this process of evaluating data starts, encouraging us to disregard data that contradict our predetermined conclusion. Motivated reasoning already has fixed the game, and genuine attempts at reason turn into mere shows of reason. Motivated reasoning leads us to prove our predetermined beliefs while disproving the beliefs of opponents.

Futurist author Robert Anton Wilson describes two main agents of motivated reasoning: the "Thinker" and the "Prover." Wilson wrote that "whatever the Thinker thinks, the Prover will prove," and that "if the Thinker thinks passionately enough, the Prover will prove the thought so conclusively that you will never talk a person out of such a belief."[27]

Skepticism is the tool that keeps the Prover in check.

Related to motivated reasoning is "special pleading," which is the tendency to excuse the beliefs that we hold dear from having to undergo skeptical review. Special pleading is what drives the double standard. It leads a Christian to believe in the Christian account of Immaculate Conception while also believing that similar stories from other traditions are absurd. Special pleading argues the following: Everyone should to be held responsible for their actions. However, my child's cheating is different because cheating is out of her character, so she deserves special treatment.

Motivated reasoning is also a characteristic that distinguishes pseudoscience from science. In science, we start with a hunch and then follow the data, wherever it leads. In pseudoscience, we start with the conclusion and select only the data that support our conclusion. In other ways, we make it look like science.

Media Lies and Spin

"Truth is hard, propaganda is cheap."[28]
— DaShanne Stokes

Falling victim to motivated reasoning is inevitable

because humans have limited capacity to process information. We must always make judgments as to what information we consider and, conversely, what information we do not consider. To manage our information intake, we select the media based on their ability to deliver information that we deem beneficial to understanding reality.

Besides the challenge to deliver useful news, there are long-standing biases that the media has always battled, such as the constant push for ratings that drives the media toward sensationalism: "If it bleeds, it leads!" There also is journalistic laziness, which encourages overly simple portrayals of a complex reality. And there are monied interests that push skewed agendas. Former U.S. Sen. Al Franken said, "The biases the media has are much bigger than conservative or liberal. They're about getting ratings, about making money, about doing stories that are easy to cover."[29]

News outlets, like individuals, have a finite capacity to process information. This limitation plays out in what to cover and what not to cover during a news cycle. Politicians have become adept at manipulating the news cycle to their purposes. Besides presenting only a skewed slice of current events, news organizations also opine during the same news segments as to how the audience should interpret the news. The important distinction between fact and interpretation blurs. This problem is exacerbated not only when the media perpetuates mistruths, but also – and even more so – when the media omits important information. The news may be factual in what it says, but also incomplete, leaving out important information. Spin is inevitable.

These various issues are often lumped together under a phrase taken from authoritarian governments: "fake news." The term suggests a hidden grand conspiracy of media outlets that are coordinating to spread news that is false. However, specific examples of this kind of fake news are rarely found. More likely, news that is critical of the narrative of those in power is dismissed as "fake news" by these authority figures. The role of the media in an open society is to hold those in power to standards of honesty and transparency. This duty can mean that the media and the government conflict, since they serve different roles in society. Such an adversarial relationship is appropriate here. If the media simply parrots only what the government tells us, that is not news. It is propaganda. As iconic newscaster Edward R. Murrow said half a century ago, "Our major obligation is not to mistake slogans for solutions."[30]

The Problem of the Internet

"About 90% of what's out there in cyberspace is hearsay – or lies – and opinion, often misinformed opinion, and it's all repeated over and over again."[31]
— David Tang

"The mind is like tofu. It tastes like whatever you marinate it in."[32]
— Sylvia Boorstein

While motivated reasoning has existed throughout history, it has become measurably – many say critically – worse with the existence of the internet. Like many communication technologies before it, the internet has an impact that is less one of type than one of degree. The internet amplifies more than it originates. It can be used as merely a broker for motivated reasoning – a powerful proving engine in which we select our beliefs, the internet "proves" them and the result is the bifurcated media environment that feeds each differing version of reality. The internet presents an unprecedented challenge to the exchange of balanced ideas. Again, it is possible for humans to be reasonable, but our default behavior is to apply our reason situationally.

Consider the speed and scope with which the internet is able to move ideas. Consider also the degree to which it allows people to construct their own reality filters and see only the ideas that they want to see. Social media sites such as Twitter, Facebook and YouTube share part of the responsibility for this problem. Sophisticated algorithms suggest content to information consumers based on past consumer behavior, assuming that people want to view things that are similar to things they have viewed in the past. As such, these suggestion engines can deliver what a person wants to see, and perhaps not what the person should see.

If your past browsing habits indicate that you are interested in hiking shoes, you are likely to be served more media – videos and ads – about outdoor equipment and hiking shoes. Likewise, if your past behavior also shows that you have an interest in an alleged conspiracy, even if the conspiracy is demonstrably false, you might – along with the hiking shoe ads – be served more content that supports the conspiracy and encourages more conspiracy thinking. The internet becomes a giant proving engine, a sophisticated and highly customizable feedback loop to which people return daily in order to reinforce their own versions of reality. Even facts can be contextualized to fit our beliefs. Lee McIntyre explains:

> In these days of 24/7 partisan cable 'news' coverage, not to mention Facebook groups, chat rooms and personal news feeds, it is increasingly possible for those who wish to do so to live in an 'information silo,' where they are seldom confronted by inconvenient facts that conflict with their favored beliefs. In this era of 'fake news' it is possible for people not only to avoid views that conflict with their own, but almost to live in an alternative reality, where their preferred views are positively reinforced and opposing views are undermined. Thus political and religious ideologies — even when they tread on empirical matters — are increasingly 'fact-free' and reflect stubborn desire to shape reality toward them.[33]

Of course, people have always been able to construct their own version of reality. Besides, joining communities of like-minded people is not – in itself – a bad thing. From small and large religious communities to political groups to survivalist groups to fringe cults such as the Peoples Temple (1954-78) and Heaven's Gate (1974-97). However, the internet has encouraged fringe groups to organize around conspiracies as never before. Think of the debunked "pizzagate" conspiracy or the QAnon conspiracy.

Long ago, George Orwell said, "If liberty means anything at all it means the right to tell people what they do not want to hear."[34] Having our beliefs challenged is an essential ingredient of an open society. The internet enables people to avoid having their views challenged. Websites post false information that is then consumed and repeated by other sites, conferring legitimacy to a falsity. False information can then rapidly "go viral." The internet encourages epistemologically closed groups, which lead to conspiracy groups.

Attempts to address this internet echo chamber are elusive, because brokering content – even what some may consider important content – for other people sets off its own alarms. Isn't such a suggestion a sort of indoctrination? Past efforts to regulate information, such as with broadcasting's fairness doctrine, have suffered their own problems, notably with the First Amendment and a reluctance to having the government determine "truth" for its citizens.

Hiking-shoe ads, news and false conspiracies are not the same types of media, so they should not be promoted as if they are simply information that internet channels have a responsibility to deliver. Recently, some social media organizations have begun experimenting with the daunting task of moderating content for its veracity so that at least the echo chamber that people construct won't be polluted with demonstrably false information. Twitter now labels some content as "false or misleading." (Recently, Twitter closed several accounts – including that of former President Donald Trump because, Twitter claimed, he used it to incite violence by spreading false information.) Facebook has started to demote, label and even remove content that includes false information. (We shouldn't underestimate the power of social media to shape opinion in society. Recently, journalist Carole Cadwalladr of The Guardian wrote, "It may turn out that Facebook isn't just bigger than China. It's bigger than capitalism."[35])

Even YouTube, which has been blamed for helping enable the resurgence of the "flat Earth" conspiracy, has experimented – with some success – in modifying its suggestion engine to identify and to demote disproven conspiracies. In an article published in Wired magazine, Clive Thompson wrote that conspiracy thinking leads to more conspiracy thinking. In one passage, he wrote:

> While one might shrug at this as marginal weirdness – *They think the Earth is flat, who cares? Enjoy the crazy, folks* – the scholarly literature finds that conspiratorial thinking often colonizes the mind. Start with flat earth, and you may soon believe Sandy Hook was a false-flag operation or that vaccines cause autism or that Q's warnings about Democrat pedophiles are a serious matter. Once you convince yourself that well-documented facts about the solar system are a fraud, why believe well-documented facts about anything?[36]

There is an argument that the best solution to reducing bad thought is the "teach a man to fish" approach: Teach people to evaluate content for themselves, largely through critical thinking. While new media may not stop us from creating our own echo chambers, maybe it can at least help to ensure that these echo chambers are not constructed out of demonstrably false information.

Patternicity

"We're wired to see patterns
like pictures in grilled cheese.
On Mars, in stars, in cliff-sides –
Oh, the things we once believed!"[37]
— Joseph Raphael Becker

Carl Jung said, "In all chaos there is a cosmos, in all disorder there is a secret order."[38] Humans are skilled at finding patterns. In fact, humans need to find patterns. We are determined to fill in blanks and to connect dots. Human beings will always strive to see an order in disorder.

A common illustration of pattern-seeking features a prehistoric hunter who is making his way across an African savannah. As he walks along the path, he continuously scans the bush for patterns that indicate something abnormal. He scans for patterns that might indicate eyes or stripes. He also listens for rustling sounds that stand out.

This ability to locate patterns is an essential survival skill. It enables the hunter to spot a crouching tiger before it pounces. When the hunter identifies and escapes this threat, he probably will survive to pass on his genes. Pattern seeking, also known as "pareidolia" or "patternicity" is an essential survival skill in nature, especially for animals that are potential prey.

Humans take pattern-seeking to extremes. We apply this skill to our language, logic and abstract thought;

when we interpret history, music, art, and more; and in every way that we attempt to make meaning. We overlay patterns over our complex environment to find or create meaning. Once we have established meaning, we complete the narrative, calling it "understanding."

Pattern-seeking also works in analogy. The thing that we do not understand is perhaps in some respect similar to the thing that we do understand. Maybe there is a connection to be made between otherwise disparate items, a similarity to be proposed and explored. By making these connections we decrease the number of things that we do not understand and increase the number of things that we do understand.

Pattern-seeking also informs our art and organizes our music. In music, we search out rhythms and melodies that evoke moods. In language, we seek understanding partly through repeated rhythm, stress, image and sound. Finding the patterns and connections is what art appreciation is all about. Finding an order in the chaos is how we make sense of nature. We lie in the grass, pointing out patterns in the clouds floating by. We are uncomfortable with – even threatened by – patternlessness.

This pattern-seeking skill also can lead to excess. Sometimes we find patterns where no meaningful pattern exists. Think of the Virgin Mary in the oil stain or the face of Elvis in the piece of toast. Think of the conspiracy theorist from popular movies, his wall plastered with newspaper articles and photographs that contain faces circled in red marker and connected together with strings of yarn. Human beings try to impose order upon disorder even in cases where there exists no order. We sometimes find a connection where there is no connection. In this pursuit, we exchange real understanding for the reassuring scratching of our evolutionary itch that leads us to identify a pattern.

Type 1 and Type 2 Errors

"There are two ways to be fooled. One is to believe what isn't true; the other is to refuse to believe what is true."[39]
— Søren Kierkegaard

Believing something that is false is only part of the problem. The other, perhaps more damaging problem arises when we do not believe something that is true.

Let's return to the pattern-seeking prehistoric man mentioned earlier. This man is walking across a Savannah on a path that borders a field of high grass. The grass provides ideal cover for hiding predators, and so the man continuously is scanning for patterns and listening for noises that may indicate a predator. We can divide this story into two types of self-deception: "Type 1" and "Type 2" errors.

A Type 1 error is a false positive. It is believing in a falsehood. In our example, this error occurs when the man's senses alert him that there is something in the bush: Maybe eyes, stripes or movement. Upon closer examination, he sees that it is only an odd configuration of leaves and a branch, along with a rustling of leaves from the wind. His heart may have raced for a moment. Perhaps adrenalin shot through his body. But, beyond this initial rush of attention, this false positive is not costly. Once he understands that there is no actual threat, he takes a deep breath and continues down the path.

Now let's discuss a Type 2 error – rejecting a truth. Pretend that there is a tiger hiding in the bush, but our man dismisses the signs as merely an odd configuration of leaves and a branch, and the rustling of leaves from the wind. Ignoring the signs, he walks on. The tiger pounces, and the man becomes prey. A Type 2 error can cost the thinker dearly. Type 2 errors explain, in part, how evolution works: The gene pool is strengthened only when the genes of the animals who don't fall victim to type 2 errors are passed forward.

Likewise, grand conspiracy theories are costly in that they distract passionate people, leading them both to worry about the wrong things (Type 1 errors) and to dismiss legitimate concerns (Type 2 errors). Thomas Huxley warned: "Irrationally held truths may be more harmful than reasoned errors."[40]

Human beings regularly see false patterns, and therefore worry about the wrong things. Mark Twain noted this when he quipped, "There has been much tragedy in my life; at least half of it actually happened."[41] We lie awake in the early hours rehearsing the economic and social catastrophes that may present themselves in the coming day. We adopt superstitions whereby we hope that wearing a lucky jersey on game days may help lead our team to victory. We're always scanning our environment for potential signs of danger, including warning signs of too much debt; social cues that signal threats; the potential terrible consequences of not being vigilant; and not paying sufficient attention. We put up with mistaking numerous false patterns in the hope that we don't fail to recognize a real danger. Millions of years of evolution have fine-tuned this trait of anxiety. Our nervousness often is considered a negative trait, but it is probably one reason humans have survived so successfully. As Stanford University neuroscientist Robert Sapolsky comments, "Essentially, we've evolved to be smart enough to make ourselves sick."[42]

We want to make sure that we do not miss serious threats and that we are scanning relevant phenomena. Yet we live in an age that is filled with threats of potentially existential Type 2 errors – such as the threat of nuclear war and the climate crisis – that we ignore to our peril. Ecologist Paul Ehrlich said, "When humanity exterminates populations and species of other creatures, it is sawing off the limb on which it is sitting, destroying working parts of our own life-support system."[43] This error is not limited to potential mass extinction through global warming and environmental destruction. It also includes mass human migration, food insecurity and an approaching fiscal cliff. And yet our mental bandwidth has limits, and when we give something our attention, we must deny something else our attention. Life can easily become a competition among things to worry about.

Both types of errors are also candidates for exploitation. Some threats are real and some imagined, but both can be leveraged by people who exploit the public fear for corporate or personal gain. Political science and politicized science are not the same thing.

Cost and Benefit

"All knowledge degenerates into probability."[44]
— David Hume

There are few beliefs that warrant our setting them in stone. Beliefs that are fixed and never subject to review should raise a red flag. The purpose of this red flag is not to reject these beliefs, but rather to review the reasons we give this belief the special privilege of being granted immunity to skepticism. "In all affairs," Bertrand Russell said, "it's a healthy thing now and then to hang a question mark on the things you have long taken for granted."[45]

Is there ever a single reason that we hold a belief? At their best, beliefs are probabilities, not certainties. Our beliefs are constructed holistically and in the context of many experiences. Therefore, we shouldn't discuss beliefs as if they were isolated on/off switches whereby we either believe them or not. Beliefs are more like the faders on a sound-mixing board, with degrees of belief that adjust in relation to other beliefs. As our experiences grow, we reevaluate these beliefs, updating our prior ones.

Like many of life's decisions, our beliefs are established largely through a cost/benefit analysis: Do the benefits of holding a belief outweigh the costs? For instance, in the crouching tiger example above, the costs of avoiding a nonexistent tiger are small, but the costs of not avoiding a real tiger can be great. The benefits of staying safe outweigh the costs of being eaten. Better safe than sorry.

A famous exercise of a cost/benefit analysis comes from the 17th-century French philosopher Blaise Pascal. In what has become known as "Pascal's Wager," he suggested that people should live as if there is a Christian God partly for cost/benefit reasons. If the Christian God does not exist, the costs of belief are small. However, if this God does exist, the costs of non-belief (eternal hell) are enormous, as are the benefits of belief (eternal heaven).

The costs and the benefits of a belief are bound to change as our knowledge and circumstances change and, more importantly, as our understanding changes. It makes no sense that we would permanently establish a belief when our understanding is always changing.

Anecdotal and Hearsay Evidence

"The plural of anecdote is not data."[46]
– Marc Bekoff

The statement "I have heard that something is true" is never as compelling as "I can show you that something is true."

Anecdotes and hearsay are the scaffolding that underly conspiracy theories. Both forms of evidence can be compelling – and even instructive – to a point. They can be useful in suggesting new starting points of investigation. However, they are poor ending points, since anecdotes and hearsay are informal information that generally cannot be verified independently or evaluated for consistency.

When anecdote or hearsay are used as comprehensive evidence, they are inherently weak. Anecdotal evidence is just that – an anecdote or a story, not a study. Hearsay evidence is little more than a rumor. In his 18th-century book "The Age of Reason," freethinker Thomas Paine bemoaned the problems of hearsay evidence – secondhand witnesses and worse – that he saw contained in the Bible: "It is hearsay upon hearsay," he wrote, "and I do not choose to rest my belief upon such evidence."[47] The evidence may command our consideration. However, it not does not demand our conclusion.

Burden of Proof

"It annoys me that the burden of proof is on us [atheists]. It should be 'You came up with the idea. Why do you believe it?' I could tell you I've got superpowers. But I can't go up to people saying 'Prove I can't fly.' They'd go: 'What do you mean, "Prove you can't fly"? Prove you can![48]*'"*
— Ricky Gervais

In any discussion that challenges the established narrative, the burden of proof – that is, who is obligated to provide evidence for their claim – generally and correctly should land on the person challenging the common narrative. This is also the case in a grand conspiracy. However, a problem with a grand conspiracy is that the burden of proof is disregarded. Its truth is assumed, not proven.

The burden of proof is just that – a burden. In a society that is organized around reasonable beliefs, we should not simply promote our beliefs without providing evidence to justify them. Every idea is not as good as every other idea. We have an obligation to provide good reasons for our beliefs, to make the case that they are more reasonable than other possible explanations.

In the context of a conspiracy, the GCTs dodge this obligation to provide evidence. If we aren't careful, the discussion then becomes a "prove me wrong" argument: For example, prove to me that the shooting massacre at Sandy Hook Elementary in 2012 wasn't simply a fake theatrical event orchestrated by then-President Barack Obama in order to take away guns; or prove to me that there was not voter fraud in an election; or prove to me that the U.S. government is not hiding UFOs; or prove to me that then-President George W. Bush did not orchestrate 9/11 as a pretext to go to war in the Middle East.

Since the grand conspiracy challenges the accepted narrative, it is therefore obligated to carry the burden of proof. British women's rights activist Annie Besant wrote:

> If my interlocutor desires to convince me that Jupiter has inhabitants, and that his description of them is accurate, it is for him to bring forward evidence in support of his contention. The burden of proof evidently lies on him; it is not for me to prove that no such beings exist before my non-belief is justified, but for him to prove that they do exist before my belief can be fairly claimed.[49]

Negotiating the burden of proof can be messy, especially in the kind of short and partial exchanges that occur online. But no one suggesting an alternate explanation is immune from the burden of proof. The more that we avoid providing reasons for our beliefs and surround ourselves with people who also escape providing reasons, the more that we should suspect our beliefs.

Anomaly hunting

"There is no such uncertainty as a sure thing."[50]
— Robert Burns

Anomaly hunting is a process by which a given narrative is repeatedly called into question with instances where data apparently contradict the overarching narrative. The motivation behind anomaly hunting is not to discover truth as much as it is to cast doubt onto the accepted narrative. The anomaly hunter presents cases in which the data do not completely explain the issue. Or she presents cases that, while explainable, still generate a feeling of doubt. But finding an anomaly is not exceptional. We should expect to find anomalies in any complex set of data. No complex situation can be explained fully. Sometimes, anomaly hunters argue that since the accepted explanation has unexplained elements, it must therefore be false. And since the official explanation is false, their reasoning follows, their alternate explanation must therefore be true.

A specific example of anomaly hunting is found in

the Sandy Hook shooting, in which a heavily armed, 20-year-old man shot his way into the school in Newtown, Conn. Before the man eventually killed himself, he had fatally shot 20 children and six adults. (Earlier that day, he also shot and killed his mother.)

Conspiracy theorists quickly seized on this event, some even claiming that the event actually was a hoax perpetrated by the government and the media in order to gin up support for a ban on assault weapons.

Disparities in the initial chaotic reports from the police and the media – disparities that are to be expected in such a situation – fueled more conspiracy thinking. One example was the initial misreport that the gun supposedly used in the shooting was found locked in the trunk of the shooter's car after he had killed himself, meaning that he couldn't possibly have used this gun in the shooting, an obvious hole in the official narrative. Even though authorities later clarified that the gun found in the locked trunk was not the gun used in the shooting, the possible crack in the narrative had already become part of a counternarrative of doubt. The clarification was interpreted by those promoting a conspiracy as only more proof of a cover-up.

Next, unscientific questions appeared about whether a gunman could shoot so many people in such a short time – questions that essentially are not answerable. But again, the questions do not need to be particularly relevant or answerable because they are intended only to cast doubt on the official story.

Then, unverified rumors and even outright falsities were asserted, such as the rumor that the agents and even the children and parents were actually paid actors who were in on the hoax.

What's noteworthy is not the veracity of any specific anomaly, but the way these anomalies, when lumped together, combine to cast doubt on the official narrative. Anomaly hunting is about a barrage of weak arguments, not the thoughtful presentation of a few solid arguments. When doubt is cast on the official narrative, it seems reasonable to replace it with an alternative narrative. Even though dozens of bad arguments do not equal one good argument, each of the dozens of bad arguments carries some evidentiary weight and can begin to sound plausible because of their sheer number.

Move the Goalposts Fallacy

Banjo: *Why has no one found the missing link between modern humans and ancient apes?*

Farnsworth: *We did find it! It's called Homo erectus!*

Banjo: *Then you have proven my case, sir, for no one has found a link between apes and this Homo erectus.*

Farnsworth: *Yes, they have! It's called Homo habilis!*

Banjo: *Ah-ha! But no one has found the missing link between ape and this so-called Homo habilis.*

Farnsworth: *Yes, they have! It's called Australopithecus africanus!*

Banjo: *Oh-ho! I've got you now! [Time Lapse. The hologram now shows 19 different species of ape.] Fair enough, but where, then, is the missing link between apes and this Darwinius masillae?*

Answer me that, professor!
Farnsworth: *Okay, granted, that one missing link is still missing...*[51]
— The TV show "Futurama"

The Moving the Goalposts Fallacy happens when a promoter of a belief satisfies the established expectations of evidence, but rather than acknowledging his fact, the person demanding the evidence changes their demand for evidence to a greater standard that has not been met. Rather than concede the issue, the person changes the rules of the game.

A classic example of the Moving the Goalposts Fallacy also comes from evolutionary theory. The opponent to evolution asks for an example of evolution happening today. The proponent might present an example drawn from macro evolution, perhaps from fruit flies or moths or diseases that have become drug resistant.

The opponent then changes the demands to see evidence to be an example of evolution happening over a long period of time.

So the evolutionist presents the fossil record or, say, an argument from genetics.

"No," says the opponent. "I need to see an example of evolution on living animals that is happening over a long period of time."

The changing demand for evidence never ends. No amount of evidence is enough. Eventually, the demand for evidence might increase so greatly that it becomes something that we cannot really expect to see in the real

Proportionality Bias

"This [proportionality bias] goes against the laws of physics stating 'for every action there is an equal and opposite reaction.' [But] This isn't physics."[52]
— Nathan McCallister

When we think of a conspiracy, often the first one to pop into our minds is the alleged conspiracy involving the assassination of President John F. Kennedy, who was shot by Lee Harvey Oswald in 1963. Questions and alternative explanations surround the event even today, over half a century later. Did Oswald act alone, or was he aided by others? Perhaps the assassination was ordered by Cuba's Fidel Castro, or the Mafia, or the CIA, or the KGB, or LBJ, or the Secret Service, or Joe DiMaggio?

The assassination has been examined and reexamined for decades. Every release of "new" documents, every new study or book, every TV documentary and every refusal to release any "secret" document still not released becomes fuel that perpetuates these various grand conspiracies. The Zapruder film, taken by a bystander which captured the assassination on film, has become the most analyzed film in history. There are numerous conspiracy theories involving the "grassy knoll," the "umbrella man," the "magic bullet."

There are many reasons, such as Kennedy's youth

and charisma, why this event has commanded attention for decades. One reason behind this continuing conspiracy is a cognitive bias called "proportionality bias." The proportionality bias speaks to our tendency to think that a large effect requires a large cause. Author Karen Sternheimer explains:

> It is not hard to believe that a powerful regime or dictator could slaughter a group of people with little or no social power, as sadly has happened over and over again in human history. But the opposite is much harder to believe: an individual or group with little power harming someone with significantly more power and status doesn't make sense. It challenges what we think we know about the social order.[53]

In the Kennedy assassination, accepting that a small and random situation led to a major event is not intuitive for many and is unacceptable to some. People doubting the official explanation continue to search for a cause that at least is proportional to its effect. Otherwise, things do not seem to match up. As screenwriter Noah Hawley said, "I think that we're pattern-seeking animals, and what we like best is a story where everything fits together, where there's no puzzle pieces left over."[54] When the cause and effect seem to be disproportional, we feel there are pieces left over.

A current manifestation of the proportionality bias is the COVID-19 coronavirus. This tiny virus has affected the entire world, causing sickness and death and economic disruption not seen in a century. For many, it is more comfortable to assume malicious intent by powerful evil agents than it is to accept that the pandemic is a random event of nature caused by a tiny virus over which our control is limited. Similarly, it is easier for some to accept that the government is extremely powerful and corrupt than it is to think that the government is perhaps not all powerful and is subject to the same randomness to which we all are subject. "There's something perversely soothing about a conspiracy theory, even one utterly malignant and diabolical, because it presupposes a world without chaos or randomness,"[55] said author Colin Dickey.

The proportionality bias speaks directly to the way humans are uncomfortable with their lack of control over the randomness in the world.

Possible Does Not Mean Probable

"Extraordinary claims require extraordinary evidence."[56]
— Carl Sagan

Every event in nature has an explanation that is the "most likely" explanation. We gather the available information and we construct a likelihood. Ideally, we take into account not just the possibility of a certain thing's being true, but also the probability of it being true.

For example, possibly there is Bigfoot. But probably there is not. Possibly the Sandy Hook shooting was a fake enactment by government conspirators. But probably it was not. Possibly a politician told a lie.

(Well, probably he did.)

We weigh these claims to decide their possibility and probability, and we determine the most likely explanation. Is it more likely that a young man entered a school and shot people or that the government, the media and the families set up a fake performance so that they could build support for a gun law?

If the probability is low, the evidence required must then be high.

In each of these cases, the possibility drives the probability. We have lots of examples of politicians lying, but not so many instances of government-instigated fake shootings. The likelihood of such an event is low.

But something that is improbable is not necessarily impossible. For example, a specific individual's winning the Powerball lottery is not at all probable, but it is completely possible. The odds are overwhelmingly low that I will win the lottery, but the odds are extremely high that somebody will win it.

Similarly, we can say that something is possible in an absurd way similar to how we might say that "anything is possible," such as the possibility that we are all living an illusion, or that Martians will invade, or that life spontaneously "happened." People promoting extraordinary explanations often like to play with the definition of what is possible. However, in the common understanding of the world, we are not living in a dream. The Martians will not invade. Life does not just happen. These things, therefore, are not commonly possible, so the expectation of evidence for them goes up appropriately.

The Arrogance of Ignorance

"These are dangerous times. Never have so many people had so much access to so much knowledge and yet have been so resistant to learning anything."[57]
—Tom Nichols

Karl Popper said, "No rational argument will have a rational effect on a man who does not want to adopt a rational attitude."[58] Most people are content to reason incompletely and are content to opine about important topics with bad reasons and limited understanding.

We are at the point in the book where explaining these biases and their remedies maxes out because these observations assume that everyone is interested in leaving their deceptions behind and in improving their thinking. In reality, many people have limited interest in accepting responsibility for their views, even on topics that are important to them. A willful ignorance is often the problem hiding beneath a simple lack of education in this information-rich world. Tom Nichols, author of "The Death of Expertise," said:

> Not only do increasing numbers of laypeople lack basic knowledge, they reject fundamental rules of evidence and refuse to learn how to make a logical argument. In doing so, they risk throwing away centuries of accumulated knowledge and undermining the practices and habits that allow us to develop new knowledge. This is more than a natural skepticism toward experts. I fear we are witnessing the death of the ideal of expertise itself.[59]

"True ignorance," Popper said, "is not the absence of knowledge, but the refusal to acquire it."[60] "A man is responsible for his ignorance,"[61] said Mulan Kundera.

In addition to this reluctance to accept that our minds might need improvement, many people are already trapped inside closed belief systems, and so changing their beliefs is especially unlikely. These people have insulated themselves from the responsibility to base their beliefs on good reasons. Author P.J. O'Rourke said, "No drug, not even alcohol, causes the fundamental ills of society. If we're looking for the source of our troubles, we shouldn't test people for drugs, we should test them for stupidity, ignorance, greed and love of power."[62]

Tying it All Together: Voter fraud in the 2020 Presidential Election

"World War 3 will be a guerrilla information war, with no division between military and civilian participation."[63]
— Marshall McLuhan

Let's take the instruments that are common in conspiracies and apply them to a specific scenario: the 2020 U.S. presidential election, specifically the allegations of massive voter fraud.

As presidential elections go, the election was not especially close. The victor, Democrat Joe Biden, won 51.3% of the vote, a majority, with 81,283,735 votes, which earned him 306 electoral votes. His opponent, incumbent President Donald Trump, a Republican, garnered 46.9% of the vote with 74,221,580 votes, or 232 electoral college votes. Nearly all polls – even long before and leading up to the election – predicted a Biden victory. So why was this election so hotly contested?

After the election, Trump immediately began alleging massive voter fraud (Trump had said even before the election that, if he did not win, he would not accept the results.) He filed dozens of lawsuits in the seven battleground states that determined the outcome of the election.

Nearly all of the dozens of the president's lawsuits (61 of 62) failed decisively in the courts. Many were dismissed, or withdrawn, or rejected on appeal. The three that were presented to the U.S. Supreme Court were rejected.

Several state recounts also found no evidence of significant fraud.

Next, governors from all 50 states certified the election results: Biden had won decidedly.

Election officials declared overwhelmingly that the election was fair and secure. The election was even characterized as the "safest in history" by security officials.[64]

Eventually, even the Department of Justice, which had been often criticized for too often doing the president's bidding, announced that there was no fraud of a magnitude that would change the outcome of the election.

Law experts called out Trump's legal team for telling the public about the abundance of evidence proving massive fraud and then telling judges (in a professional and ethically accountable environment) that they actually had no real evidence.

Throughout this process of gathering data, the evidence did not fundamentally change. There were no "bombshells" or courtroom verdicts that uncovered irregular corruption. In fact, the two big developments seemed to be the growing lack of evidence and the more erratic behavior of the incumbent's legal team.

Still, Trump continued to repeat the narrative that the election had been stolen, even claiming that he actually had won the election "by a landslide."

Once the standard remedies – the court cases, recount initiatives and investigations – were exhausted, the Trump administration began a legislative effort to interrupt with the hope to eventually overturn the certification of electoral votes. Even the idea of declaring martial law reportedly was discussed.

How did this conspiracy claiming there was massive fraud continue to grow in the number of believers, even when the evidence seemed to establish clearly that no systemic fraud existed? We can now apply the cognitive traps and fallacies specific to this situation.

The first trap was a display of confirmation bias where, as Francis Bacon said, we "observe when a thing hits, but not when it misses." Trump's words challenged the considered judgments of courts, election officials, state governors, congresspeople, law enforcement bodies and international observers. All such judgments were ignored by the president and his team. Instead, anecdotes, rumors, allegations and affidavits of isolated incidents of fraud – such as a single individual attempting to vote twice – were seized on as evidence that a vast conspiracy had taken place.

The second trap was motivated reasoning, starting with the premise that that there was a massive, organized fraud. Because this was not a mission intended to establish truth, but rather a mission to find fraud, regardless of the evidence. The Thinker determined there was fraud, and the Prover was sent out to find it.

We should expect to see some irregularities in any sizable election, including isolated cases of fraud. However, in the case of the 2020 election, in an intense case of anomaly hunting, every irregularity was cited as one more example of massive fraud. In the face of overwhelming contrary evidence, Trump and his team began to overload the news not only with promises of massive evidence, but with numerous anecdotes, allegations and unverified rumors intended to cast doubt on the electoral process.

Interestingly, the more pieces of evidence that appeared disproving the conspiracy, the more each piece of evidence seemed to carry less influence, as though the preponderance of evidence disproving a conspiracy actually made this evidence less effective. So, while one or two lost court cases might be significant and taken seriously, dozens of lost court cases seemed only to prove the cover-up.

Unfounded allegations were brought of corrupt election officials, politicians and the media; of legal votes not counted and illegal votes counted; of interference by countries such as Germany and Venezuela, or by George Soros or other "leftist operatives"; of widespread corruption targeting Trump and his family; of numerous hacked voting machines that had changed votes for Trump into votes for Biden; of mysterious drops in the night of thousands of ballots for Biden, or mysterious suitcases and U-Haul trucks filled with ballots for Biden; of ballots found in dumpsters; of votes dismissed because voters incorrectly used Sharpie pens; of fake votes by deceased people, illegal aliens and children; of huge numbers of votes that appeared from nowhere or under the cover of night; and of Trump election monitors who were refused access to observe vote counters.

Such allegations provided only the promise of evidence. As we have said, the weight of just one of these allegations does not amount to much. It was the combined effect that mattered. The GCT is not interested in bringing up issues so that they can be addressed in a systematic, orderly and judicial way. Rather, in a lesson drawn from history, if you tell a lie that's big enough and tell it frequently enough, it will be believed. Those alleging a conspiracy repeated the many weak arguments which were then brought up in quick succession. Maybe, they thought, the sheer number of spurious arguments would be mistaken for a few strong arguments.

Eventually, the conspiracy became a closed belief system, where no reasonable evidence could falsify the claim of a voter fraud conspiracy. In fact, it seemed like the more evidence that emerged pointing to a fair election, the more the argument alleging fraud seemed to gain traction.

At the same time, ad hominem attacks ran rampant.

Trump threatened, insulted or shamed anyone advancing the narrative that the election was fair. Notably, Georgia's secretary of state, Republican Brad Raffensperger, was threatened over his continued insistence that the election was fair. On a call with Raffensperger, Trump and his campaign team pleaded with Raffensperger to find votes that might overturn the election. When Raffensperger refused, he was threatened again.[65] Cybersecurity and Infrastructure Security Agency Director Chris Krebs, who had stated that the election was among the most secure in history, was fired Nov 17.[66] Numerous other people were criticized either for being dupes for not seeing the conspiracy or, worse, for being knowing participants in the conspiracy. Top Michigan election official Jocelyn Benson had armed supporters of the president march outside her home.[67] Attorney General William Barr was fired (or resigned, depending on who is telling the story) for disagreeing with Trump about voter fraud. Still, the "massive voter fraud" conspiracy continued to gain traction in some groups.

As legal routes through which Trump could present his case were exhausted, the burden of proof was shifted, so that rather than his team having to prove that massive voter fraud had occurred, he acted as though "everyone knows" about the massive fraud. Massive fraud was now assumed. As lawsuits and recounts failed to uncover any substantial voter fraud, the president's team tried to shift the burden of proof, insisting that the Biden administration could not enter the White House until they had proven that there was no fraud.[68]

Next, the fraud conspiracy did what grand conspiracies do: It widened the list of conspirators. The list now included state election monitors; the entire Democratic Party; the entire "mainstream" media; foreign countries; voting machine companies; various state courts and governors; the FBI and the CIA; the Department of Justice; the judicial branch of the government, including the Supreme Court; the Chinese parts of voting machines; and more than two dozen international observers. For many, the conspiracy began to crumble under its own weight. But, unfortunately, not for everyone. Even though the allegations had failed the evidence test at every step, tens of millions of people still believed these allegations of systemic fraud.

On Jan. 6, 2021, the day Congress was formalizing Biden's victory, the defeated president was addressing a crowd of protesters that he had called to rally Washington, D.C. In a display of outrage over the formalization, the group turned violent. They marched to the Capitol, overran Capitol Police and smashed their way into the building. Congressional members meeting at the time were rushed to a protected area. Vice President Mike Pence was whisked away. One police officer and four protesters died. The Capitol building was damaged, vandalized and desecrated. Exactly a week later, Trump was impeached by the House of Representatives for "Incitement of Insurrection."

Eventually, on Jan. 20, Biden was inaugurated as the new president. The inauguration, surrounded by National Guard Troops, was uneventful. Troops had also been deployed to every state capitol in the fear of more disruptions.

Because believers in the conspiracy had inoculated themselves from falsification, the overwhelming amount of evidence proving that there was no large-scale voter fraud stopped having much effect. This series of events, which is an example of the dangers of a grand conspiracy theory, highlights the cost and seriousness of insulating oneself from the facts. Apple CEO Tim Cook said in a speech after the Capitol riot:

> What are the consequences of prioritizing conspiracy theories and violent incitement simply because of the high rates of engagement? What are the consequences of not just tolerating but rewarding content that undermines public trust in life-saving vaccinations? What are the consequences of seeing thousands of users joining extremist groups and then perpetuating an algorithm that recommends even more? It is long past time to stop pretending that this approach doesn't come with a cost. A polarization of lost trust, and yes, of violence. A social dilemma cannot be allowed to become a social catastrophe.[69]

Besides the initial disorientation that Biden's inauguration brought to conspiracists, many fear the conspiracy probably will not die out, but is likely to re-emerge in the future.

CHAPTER SEVEN
Going Forward

Be Reasonable

"Those who invalidate reason ought seriously to consider whether they argue against reason with or without reason."[1]
—Ethan Allen

HUMAN BEINGS ENJOY A remarkable gift of reason. However, the last half dozen centuries have revealed that we are not highly rational beings that approach the world armed with logic and reason. We do not use reason consistently. Nor do we always use these tools instinctively. Never do we use reason perfectly.

Humans are exceptional in our ability to override our natural passions with reason, but our having to override our natural passions implies that using reason is not our default behavior. Our default behavior is to choose intuition and self-interest over reason, choosing the Oreo over the carrot, even when we know this may not be the best choice. Reason is a skill that requires development and practice.

We have taken a look at how our minds work – and do not work. This chapter does not suggest a cure to sloppy thinking, but only strategies to help us guard against our worse cognitive tendencies. They are remedies to Francis Bacon's concept of "Idols of the Tribe," the cognitive deceptions inherent to our species.

The Duty to Assume Good Intent

"Do nothing out of selfish ambition or vain conceit, but in humility consider others better than yourselves."
— Philippians 2:3

Baruch Spinoza said, "I have labored carefully not to mock, lament, or execrate, but to understand, human actions."[2] The default behavior of humans when navigating the natural world is to settle into groups based on beliefs and culture that are similar to ours. This preference is understandable – choosing the comfort, safety and stability of our like-minded associations over others. We look to our in-group for safety, compassion and empathy.

However, the process of defining our in-group also works to define the out-group, and defining the out-group is another human characteristic. In fact, this "Us vs. Them" behavior comes even more naturally than does our desire to get along, since defending our in-group against an outside threat has the more obvious payoff of safety than does making our in-group more inclusive to those that we consider outsiders.

Religion, politics and even sports quickly can devolve into tribalistic behavior, our animalistic, "chimp" side. (After all, we share more than 95% of chimpanzee DNA.) Sociologist Jonathan Haidt identifies tribal loyalty as one of the five primary foundations of morality among humans:

> Morality binds and blinds. It binds us into ideological teams that fight each other as though the fate of the world depended on our side winning each battle. It blinds us to the fact that each team is composed of good people who have something important to say.[3]

Aldous Huxley said, "The propagandist's purpose is to make one set of people forget that certain other sets of people are human."[4] It is naive to think we are not the victims of propaganda already. We should assume that we already are infected by propaganda, and that sometimes we work to dehumanize those humans who simply disagree with us. We should realize that other people, too, are probably victims of propaganda. Consequently, they are likely to approach us with the same zero-sum mentality with which we approach them.

Because creating division often comes more naturally than does creating unity, skepticism turned inward is desperately needed here. Identifying what unites us is a useful first step in understanding what divides us. Rather than immediately "circling the wagons" and diving straight into ad hominem attacks, we should take a breath and enter into discussions first by identifying areas of commonality, such as shared values and desires. The Austrian poet Rainer Maria Rilke wrote:

> I live my life in widening circles
> that reach out across the world.
> I may not complete this last one
> but I will give myself to it.[5]

The goal is not to win an argument, to change a mind or to defend a belief as much as it is to understand what built the belief. Realizing that other people are driven by basic human values and that they are also probably victims of propaganda (just as we are) can be two items on our mental checklist to which we refer before we enter into discussions of controversy. We bring our best selves to a respectful discussion, one in which we recognize that everyone wants to thrive.

Assuming good intent is important regarding conspiracy thinking. As Jonathan Swift said, "It is useless to attempt to reason a man out of a thing he was never reasoned into."[6] Bottom line: The GCT is only trying to make sense of reality, and as is the case with all human beings, reason probably plays only a supporting role in this effort. Conspiracy thinking is about belonging, controlling and having power. Trying to out-argue a conspiracy theorist is going to have limited effect. Instead, we should display empathy and ask probing, sincere questions such as "Can you help me understand how this works?" Questions like that carry no judgment; rather, they encourage the GCT to think through their assumptions. As we have said, listening is key to understanding. Talking is not the best way to understand. As Spinoza said, "The endeavor to understand is the first and only basis of virtue."[7] The endeavor to persuade comes somewhere far down the list.

The Duty Not to Deceive Ourselves

"It's easier to fool people than to convince them that they have been fooled."[8]
— Mark Twain

We should be wary of beliefs that offer no way for us to prove them false. We easily mistake not proving a thing false with proving that thing true; just because we have not disproven a thing does not mean that we have proven it. One of the most famous quotations about the scientific method comes from physicist Richard Feynman. As quoted earlier, he said, "Science is a way of trying not to fool yourself. The principle is that you must not fool yourself, and you are the easiest person to fool."[9]

While not fooling ourselves is the principle rule for scientific progress, it also applies very much to developing healthy beliefs. Because we easily default to believing what we prefer to believe regardless of the data and because we follow our passions more readily than we follow our reasoning, we must take special care not to deceive ourselves. Skeptic and magician Penn Jillette said, "If there's something you really want to believe, that's what you should question the most."[10]

As we have stated, this does not mean that our beliefs are not true, but it does suggest that we do well to ensure that we are not to simply doing what many people across the world do, which is to start with the assumption that our beliefs are the right ones and then cover these identifying beliefs with any proof that we can find.

As is the case with a pilot performing a pre-flight check, where she evaluates all the systems in her aircraft to ensure that they are functioning properly, there is a "pre-belief" checklist of questions to ask ourselves before we believe something.

First, there are questions that concern the source of the information: Is the source credible? Reliable? Biased? Who stands to gain from presenting this information? Who is paying for this news source?

Second, we can ask about the information itself: Is the information corroborated with other reliable sources? Is it balanced, representing other valid points of view? Is the information consistent with other sources? Does it address alternate viewpoints? Is it logical? Is it reasonable? Is it factual? (Facts are not spinnable. Usually, we can define a fact as something to which both sides of an issue would agree.)

Third, there are questions regarding the emotional appeals being used: Why is this news catching my attention? Is the headline sensational? Is the language extreme? Is the language more emotional than logical? Is the message divisive or unifying? Does it suggest a positive agenda, or does it just attempt to create a negative impression about someone or something? Are these reasons that I should be especially skeptical?

When we look at all the various ways to live in the world, all the places to be born, all the different cultures and faiths, and all the things to believe, we do well to ask ourselves this: What are the odds that I just happened to be born into the truest version of life? Perhaps we were born into the truest version of life. But probably we were not, and we just are drifting along in a sea of confirmation bias that is founded not in facts, but in our tendency to promote our own stories. We should not become victim of our strong urge to believe.

The Duty to Have Good Reasons

"A wise man, therefore, proportions his belief to the evidence."[11]
— David Hume

What is evidence but a collection of good reasons?

Facts are bits of evidence, and logic and reason are the processes we use to connect them together to create meaning. The problem is that authority and tradition can also feel like evidence. But authority and tradition are at best weak evidence; Rarely are they good reasons to believe something. More likely, they are a sign that our beliefs were passively inherited rather than actively developed.

For the most part, belief is the rule, while skepticism remains the exception. Bertrand Russell said, "Man is a credulous animal, and must believe something; in the absence of good grounds for belief, he will be satisfied with bad ones."[12] Beliefs rooted in tradition or authority are especially problematic because they can occupy a privileged place in our reality that makes them resistant to scrutiny, skepticism or reason.

Because of our default tendency to believe something that is appealing, no matter the evidence, we should take care not to mistake beliefs that are merely comfortable for beliefs that are well reasoned. If we make this mistake, we are likely to preserve the folly, regardless of its veracity. If our beliefs lack compelling reasons, if we are choosing thoughtless certainty over thoughtful skepticism, then we should take a step back, examine our intuitions and our motivations, and reexamine the data.

The Duty to Doubt Energetically

"Modest doubt is call'd the beacon of the wise."[13]
— William Shakespeare

Will Durant said, "No one deserves to believe unless he has served an apprenticeship in doubt."[14] It turns out that the essential ingredient in building a solid foundation of knowledge is the same ingredient that we resist most: doubt.

"What we need is not the will to believe, but the wish to find out,"[15] said the poet William Wordsworth. Bertrand Russell expounded on this sentiment with the following:

> William James used to preach the 'will-to-believe.' For my part, I should wish to preach the 'will-to-doubt.' None of our beliefs are quite true; all have at least a penumbra of vagueness and error. The methods of increasing the degree of truth in our beliefs are well known; they consist in hearing all sides, trying to ascertain all the relevant facts,

> controlling our own bias by discussion with people who have the opposite bias, and cultivating a readiness to discard any hypothesis which has proved inadequate. These methods are practiced in science, and have built up the body of scientific knowledge ... In science, where alone something approximating to genuine knowledge is to be found, [its] attitude is tentative and full of doubt.[16]

If faith is the assurance of things not seen, skepticism is the doubt of these things. Doubt is the essential ingredient of modern philosophy. Descartes, often referred to as the father of modern doubt, said, "If you would be a real seeker after truth, it is necessary that at least once in your life you doubt, as far as possible, all things."[17]

Every belief that is foundational to us should come under an aggressive scrutiny at some point in our lives. We should ask ourselves this: What would convince me that I am wrong? Sometimes, the answer is Nothing would persuade me that I am wrong. In these cases, we should not be surprised that, no matter what type of evidence we see, we stick to these beliefs. We may stick to them merely because we have excused them from any kind of scrutiny.

The Duty to Be Skeptical and Not Cynical

"Be shrewd as serpents and innocent as doves."
— Matthew 10:16

Living in a world of doubt is not the purpose of life. We strive to always be skeptical, never cynical. Doubt is only the first step toward belief, the first step toward certitude. "If a man will begin with certainties, he shall end in doubts," said Francis Bacon, "but if he will be content to begin with doubts, he shall end in certainties."[18]

However, as we have seen, an ill-informed doubt is ultimately as dangerous than an ill-informed belief. Upton Sinclair said, "It is foolish to be convinced without evidence, but it is equally foolish to refuse to be convinced by real evidence."[19] Remaining unpersuaded in the face of compelling evidence is one of Søren Kierkegaard's two ways to fool yourself: not believing in something that is true. (That is the "Type 2" error that we discussed earlier.)

Sowing doubt and mistrust is a strategy used by politicians and religious leaders in their efforts to extract obedience from their followers. These "merchants of doubt" – as Naomi Oreskes, co-author of the book with the same name, refers to them – promote doubt, mistrust and cynicism and then lead people with the help of this division. They undermine common values and cast doubt on our institutions: Does smoking *really* cause cancer? Can you *really* trust the media? The government? The other side?

Fortunately, the best cure for cynical doubt is intelligent doubt. This rigorous skepticism produces the kind of certainty that comes only from establishing beliefs that have risen through doubt.

The Duty to Accept Responsibility for Our Beliefs

"No one man's belief is in any case a private matter which

concerns himself alone."[20]
— William Kingdon Clifford

A common saying is "The thought manifests the word, and the word manifests the deed." Gandhi said "A man is but a product of this thoughts. What he thinks, he becomes."[21] Our beliefs matter. They determine how we organize our lives. Our deeds eventually define ourselves and, to an extent, our environment. Because belief creates behavior, we have an obligation to ensure that our beliefs are reasonable – not just for ourselves and for our families, but for the larger community. The larger community is bound not only to benefit from our good beliefs, but to suffer because of our bad beliefs. As Voltaire said, "Those who can make you believe absurdities can make you commit atrocities."[22] Therefore, just as with properly disposing of our trash, insuring our automobile or isolating ourselves when we have a potentially infectious fever, we have a communal obligation – an epistemic responsibility – to ensure that our own beliefs are healthy and reasonable so that they can assist in building a healthy and strong community.

George Santayana praised reason, as "man's imitation of divinity."[23] Reason is often cited by many as nature's crowning achievement. Others boast that reason is what separates humanity from other animals. Even those skeptical of reason make this judgment by using reason. In order for us to become our best selves, we should develop our reason.

Santayana also warned that even though reason may be our most divine attribute, it is not our strongest faculty: "Habit is stronger than reason."[24] As success coach Darren Hardy said, "Old habits eat good intentions for lunch."[25] Reason certainly is a great thing that we can do, and yet often it is not the natural thing that we do. Reason is not something that simply happens to humans. Reason is a learned skill. It is an elective, not a requirement. Perpetuating and protecting weak beliefs also can become a habit. Holding a sloppy belief makes it easier for us to hold other sloppy beliefs. William Kingdon Clifford said, "Every time we let ourselves believe for unworthy reasons, we weaken our powers of self-control, of doubting, of judicially and fairly weighing evidence."[26] Because people more naturally arrive at poor beliefs than good ones, it is imperative that we develop our capacity to reason.

Also, we should not let the sloppy reasoning of others go unchallenged. No one is entitled to be ignorant, since sloppy thinking leads to a sloppy reality that decreases the quality of life for everyone. Enabling the poor reasoning of our friends and our collective tribe allows them to escape a crucial obligation we have to society of thinking with rigor, of not offending reason. We discussed earlier that the media too often blends news, facts and opinion. Lee McIntyre said,

> At a day in age where scientific results are at our fingertips, we all bear some responsibility for the warrant behind our empirical beliefs. And, for science, it is a problem either way. Whether someone has lit the fire of denialism, or simply is stopping by to warm their hands, it is still repudiation of a core value of science.[27]

Still, we are responsible for our ignorance. We are responsible for the bad ideas that we hold and spread. Philosophers have long promoted the idea that ignorance is not without its victims. Belief is a communal responsibility. Clifford said:

> But if the belief has been accepted on insufficient evidence, the pleasure is a stolen one. Not only does it deceive ourselves by giving us a sense of power which we do not really possess, but it is sinful, because it is stolen in defiance of our duty to mankind.[28]

One advantage to living in a free society is that we live in a marketplace of ideas and are hardly forced to get our information from a single source. We can control the information that we consume. Indeed, it is our responsibility to control it responsibly. In the 2020 documentary, "Things I Wish I Knew Before I Started Talking," TV and radio host Michael Smirconish characterized the type of media that has become prevalent on social media and television as the modern version of pro wrestling: "Entertainment masked as news, constant conflict, good guys versus bad guys, and preordained outcomes. …Good for ratings. Good for revenue. Bad for the country" Smirconish added: "When politicians take their cues from the pro wrestling of the modern era, the nation suffers. Our climate can't – won't – improve until we do something about that, and in order for that to happen more people need to change the channel."[29]

The Duty to Believe Slowly, Then Enthusiastically

"This is how philosophers should salute each other: 'Take your time.'"[30]
— Ludwig Wittgenstein

For most topics that lead to belief, there is little cost in not taking a position. For other topics, however, withholding judgment comes with a high social cost, and professing a belief can be as much a loyalty test as it is a question of sincere belief. Still, as stoic philosopher Marcus Aurelius said, belief is a personal matter that no one can force – specifically, "It is in our power to have no opinion about a thing."[31]

Issues that are insoluble do not require an expression of belief or non-belief. Denis Diderot quipped that there are topics where it is unnecessary to express an opinion: "It is very important not to mistake hemlock for parsley; but not at all so to believe or not in God."[32]

When we are encouraged to profess a belief before we have sufficient evidence, we are being invited to embrace the bias and to begin walking down the path of motivated reasoning. This is the instant where we take the leap from evidence to faith, where we replace data with dogma. Once we begin down this path, it is hard to reverse. "The less there is to justify a traditional custom, the harder it is to get rid of it,"[33] said Mark Twain.

Society rewards certainty, and it views uncertainty as a weakness. Society urges us to quickly pronounce belief regarding specific insoluble questions such as the existence of God, as though these ideas are shy and fragile, and may become damaged if we consider them too directly, too thoroughly or too slowly. However, doubt happens to be the best route humans have to arrive at a stable degree of certainty, and therefore doubt should be embraced. Galileo said, "to believe slowly is the strength of wisdom."[34] We can carefully and fully consider an idea without having to accept it. But a benefit of withholding judgment is that when conviction comes, it is real conviction, not simply the appearance of conviction.

This epistemic responsibility – the responsibility for what we believe – also works both ways: Just as we have a moral obligation to commit to an idea once the evidence warrants it, we have a moral obligation to not commit too quickly just because our culture or tribe expects it.

The Duty to Discuss Difficult Topics
"The growth of knowledge depends entirely upon disagreement."[35]
— Karl Popper

Just as science is a process, not a destination, the discussion of difficult ideas also is a process, not a destination. Because our understanding of reality always will be open-ended, the need for civil discussion will never go away. It is a common refrain that it is inappropriate to discuss politics and religion in polite company. I disagree. The goal is not to avoid these discussions but rather to discuss them regularly and respectfully, using mutually agreed upon rules of reason, respect and evidence. As citizens of a free and open society, we have an obligation to discuss even difficult issues. This obligation applies even to topics that are seemingly insoluble. We continually improve our discussions through the practice of defending them in an environment of goodwill.

Through repeated attempts at discussion and understanding, we get better at avoiding falling victim to fallacies such as scarecrow and ad hominem. We get better also at not falling victim to cognitive traps. We become comfortable with the idea that good people can disagree about ideas. We practice virtues such as respect, self-control, accuracy, patience, connection, tact and humility. We develop our listening skills. Importantly, we learn that winning an argument or persuading a person is not as important as understanding and connecting.

We should not let bad ideas pass unchallenged just because they might lead to difficult discussions or because the topics are too dear for us to discuss critically. The cost of reticence here is that we become victims to the weak beliefs of others, as well as of our own, since they remain unchallenged.

One of the disciplines that the ancient Greeks left us is the practice of "dialectic." Dialectic addresses the reality that hearing varied opinions is an inevitable and welcome aspect of an open society. How do we welcome this reality? We do so through the skill of dialectic. Here are the three goals of dialectic: to help us learn more about the specific subject we are discussing; to clearly expose weak arguments and errors in belief regarding the subject; and to allow us better at discussing topics of disagreement.

As a society, we are not going to improve our skills regarding discussing difficult topics by not discussing them. Author Christopher Hitchens said, "You may not be interested in the dialectic but the dialectic is interested in you; you can't give up politics, it won't give you up."[36] Regarding science, Mario Livio said discussing difficult topics is essential today, as these topics are potentially existential:

> As Galileo's case (and, indeed, those of Darwin, Einstein, and other scientists) have demonstrated, we should trust the science – the stakes are simply too high not to. We can, and should, have a serious discussion on precisely what to do in order to address the consequences of scientific discoveries, such as the threats posed by climate change (for example, rising sea levels and the dramatic increase in the frequency of extreme weather events).[37]

If you don't feel like a study of classical dialectic, consider reading the bestselling book, "Crucial Conversations: Tools for Talking When Stakes Are High." The authors write, "At the core of every successful conversation, lies the free flow of relevant information."[38] Just because people often are awful when they discuss politics and religion does not mean they will always be awful. This is only a lack of practice. Let's practice by doing.

The Duty to be Consistent

"I don't believe in astrology; I'm a Sagittarius and we're skeptical."[39]
— Arthur C. Clarke

The greatest single trap regarding belief is that people apply their critical thinking skills inconsistently.

Several cognitive traps are involved in this inconsistency. There is confirmation bias – where we promote the information that supports our beliefs while demoting information that runs contrary to them. There is motivated reasoning – where our efforts to interpret the world are not driven by a desire to understand, but rather by a desire to prove our preferences. There is special pleading – where we excuse our select beliefs from the normal intellectual scrutiny that we demand from others.

It is not enough to simply be skeptical of other people's beliefs. We all have witnessed people who are skeptical in their critique of the beliefs of others but are either incapable or unwilling to turn that skepticism on their own beliefs. We also have to be skeptical of our own. The best bit of cognitive hygiene we can perform is to be consistent in how we apply our critical thinking. Writer and comedian Tim Minchin said:

> We must think critically, and not just about the ideas of others. Be hard on your beliefs. Take them out onto the verandah and beat them with a cricket bat.... Be intellectually rigorous. Identify your biases, your prejudices, your privilege.[40]

The more we believe something, the more skeptical we should be. "Let every student of nature," said Francis Bacon, "take this as a rule: that whatever his mind seizes and dwells upon with peculiar satisfaction is to be held in suspicion."[41] If we have trouble applying skepticism to our own beliefs, then consistency demands that we are equally generous with the beliefs of others, giving their beliefs the same breaks as we give ours. For instance, if we believe that faith is a valid path to truth, then we are obligated to extend this belief consistently to the believers of other faith traditions.

The Duty to Ask Good Questions

"It is not the answer that enlightens, but the question."[42]
— Eugene Ionesco

There is a legend about a computer programmer who kept a rock the size of his hand sitting on the shelf in his office. Whenever he had a programming question, he would hold up the rock, gaze at it attentively as if it were a skull, and thoughtfully and aloud ask the rock the question. Often, upon hearing himself verbalize the question, he would ascertain the answer. Socrates said that understanding a question is half of the answer. Targeted questions that are rightly asked advance the discussion. As with a good theory, good questions uncover more good questions, whereas an answer that does not generate more questions simply closes down discussion. Richard Paul and Linda Elder write that it is not possible to be a good thinker and a poor questioner:

> Because we cannot be skilled at thinking unless we

are skilled at questioning, we strive for a state of mind in which essential questions become second nature. They are the keys to productive thinking, deep learning, and effective living.[43]

Asking good questions also is a learned skill that requires attentiveness, focus and engaged listening.

The Duty to Listen for Understanding

"One of the best ways to persuade others is with your ears – by listening to them."[44]
— Dean Rusk

Making sure that we are understood is usually our No. 1 priority when engaging in an argument. Making sure that we understand the other person falls somewhere down the list. How common is it that, while our opponent is expressing themselves, our minds are busy composing our next response instead of actively listening?

Listening and asking questions model engagement, and also lead to real understanding. Listening also ensures that we are responding to the other person's arguments and not simply changing the subject with our own arguments. "People almost never change without first feeling understood,"[45] said Douglas Stone, author of "Difficult Conversations: How to Discuss What Matters Most." Listening is especially important in a discussion about an alleged conspiracy, since the belief is often about being understood as much as it is about evidence. Listening is half of communication. Often, it is the better half. It is impossible to learn anything while we are talking, when we are the only person doing the teaching. Therefore, we "seek first to understand, then to be understood."[46]

We can practice our listening skills by "mirroring," where a person starts their reply not by reiterating their arguments for the seventh time – perhaps with increased volume and more precise enunciation – but by repeating their opponent's argument back to them. This practice shows our opponent that they have been heard correctly and have been taken seriously. Mirroring also helps us improve our self-control. It lowers the temperature when the discussion gets heated. Most important, it helps us understand.

Science and Democracy

"Science is far from a perfect instrument of knowledge. It's just the best one we have. In this respect, as in many others, it's like democracy."[47]
— Carl Sagan

"A constitutional democracy is in serious trouble if its citizenry does not have a certain degree of education and civic virtue."[48]
— Phillip E. Johnson

United States Supreme Court Associate Justice Robert Jackson said, "It is not the function of our government to keep the citizen from falling into error; it is the function of the citizen to keep the government from falling into error."[49] Ensuring that our beliefs are well founded is important in society, and especially important in a democracy, where bad beliefs can easily translate to bad public policy. We have the responsibility to keep our thinking healthy so we can ensure that our government remains healthy.

Science has fared well in democracies because in both systems there is a sentiment that people adjust themselves to the evidence, rather than adjusting the evidence to themselves.

Authors Steven Scapin and Simon Schaffer said, "Solutions to the problem of knowledge are solutions to the problem of social order."[50] In a democracy, the method that we use to correct and improve – i.e., the election process – determines the quality of our government. We vote out bad politicians, and hopefully replace them with better ones.

In science, adherence to the scientific method determines the quality of a theory, and therefore our explanations of reality. Using the scientific method, through testing, we replace false elements of a theory with new, hopefully more true ones.

Both systems have built into them the ability to continuously improve. Both systems self-correct. Both systems recognize they are always a work in progress. After all, in a democracy the goal is a *more* perfect union, not a perfect union. Likewise, in science, the goal is a more perfect understanding. A perfect understanding is not expected. Both systems function best when there is a multiplicity of ideas, free inquiry and free expression. Furthermore, institutionalized skepticism is built into each system. In a democracy, this skepticism is made manifest in the form of an opposition government and a free press. In reasonable thinking, it manifests in the free flow of ideas – and the humility to consider them.

A Note on Language: Language Reflects Perception

"Words are not trivial. They matter because they raise consciousness."[51]
— Richard Dawkins

In his book "The Language Instinct: How the Mind Creates Language," author Stephen Pinker lists several identifying characteristics of animals: Spiders spin webs. Bats navigate with sonar. An identifying characteristic of people is that we use symbols to communicate. We cannot help it. Pinker said: "Humans are so innately hardwired for language that they can no more suppress their ability to learn and use language than they can suppress the instinct to pull a hand back from a hot surface."[52] Language determines how we see the world and, just as we don't know what we don't know, we only understanding a thing to the degree that we have the vocabulary to describe it. "The limits of my language mean the limits of my world,"[53] said Ludwig Wittgenstein. In language, words are created and adapted to describe each new experience of reality. (Conversely, words fall out of use once they are no longer useful in communicating our experience.)

For example, the first mention of the word "scientist" came in 1833. Galileo used a term more akin to "natural philosopher," which means a person who studies the natural world. Because the word "scientist" was missing, the role of one was also vague. Science historian David Wootton said, "A revolution in ideas requires a revolution in language. It is thus simple to test the claim that there was a Scientific Revolution in the seventeenth century by looking for the revolution in language that must have accompanied it."[54] In the period of the scientific revolution we can see the language grow to accommodate the new movement. One way we can point to a scientific revolution is to trace scientific words. We see a variety of new words – or also old words with new definitions – such as "fact," "theory," "experiment," "hypothesis" and "evidence."

We cannot overestimate the extent to which language drives and also reflects human progress. We aren't especially strong, fast or lethal (at least on an individual level). But our ability to use symbols makes us especially good at cooperation and at communicating knowledge to one another both now and, through the written word, to future generations.

Philosophical Razors

Philosophical razors are guideposts to keeping our thinking clear. They eliminate – shave off, as it were, like a razor – unhelpful, even harmful processes.

Here are the nine common philosophical razors:

Occam's razor

We mentioned this razor earlier. It is the guiding principle that the most simple explanation is probably the correct one. This is the general rule, but our discoveries of deep nature have often shown that this rule can break down. After we consider all the data the simplest explanation is probably the correct explanation.

Sagan's razor
"Extraordinary claims require extraordinary evidence." This razor often is used in explanations that require the supernatural or other baroque explanations for phenomena.

Hume's razor
"Causes must be sufficiently able to produce the effect assigned to them." Hume's razor says causes must be able to produce the effect. If it cannot produce the effect, then either we throw out the explanation or we add elements to it to make it adequate.

Hitchens' razor
"What can be asserted without evidence can be dismissed without evidence." This is from the Latin maxim "Quod gratis asseritur, gratis negatur."

Duck's razor
"If it looks like a duck, swims like a duck, and quacks like a duck, then it probably is a duck." If all the data is pointing a certain direction, then we should strongly consider accepting the explanation.

Popper's falsifiability razor
"Every genuine test of a theory is an attempt to

falsify it, or refute it." We covered this earlier, discussing what makes a good theory. For a theory to be considered scientific, it must be possible to disprove or refute it. If it is not open to refutation, then we can assume that it is not true. This razor criticizes bad theories, religious doctrine and conspiracy theories.

Newton's flaming laser razor

"If something cannot be settled by experiment, it is not worth debating." This is a nod to Newton's contention that the experimental process has enormous power with which to explain our environment.

Grice's razor

"Meaning is to be found in semantic context of a statement, over the literal meaning." This razor concerns context. For instance, if you dump a glass of ice water over my head, and I exclaim, "I'm gonna kill you!", the literal meaning of what I said is probably not the correct or contextual meaning. We consider the true meaning over the literal meaning.

Hanlon's razor

"Never attribute to malice that which can be adequately explained by incompetence or stupidity." Sometimes, things happen out of random events of stupidity, incompetence or unawareness. We should not assume bad intent without first considering simple incompetence.

Everything is an Experiment

"Every aspect of life is an experiment that can be better understood if it is perceived in that way."[1]
— John Brockman

In his book "The Demon-Haunted World: Science as a Candle in the Dark," Carl Sagan delivers his famous dictum that everything is an experiment:

> Every act of Congress, every Supreme Court decision, every Presidential National Security Directive, every change in the Prime Rate is an experiment. Every shift in economic policy, every increase or decrease in funding for Head Start, every toughening of criminal sentences is an experiment. Exchanging needles, making condoms freely available, or decriminalizing marijuana are all experiments. ...Privatizing mental health care or prisons is an experiment. ...Handguns are available for self-protection in Seattle, but not in nearby Vancouver, Canada; handgun killings are five times more common and the handgun suicide rate is ten times greater in Seattle. Guns make impulsive killing easy. This is also an experiment.[2]

All humans are scientists. The only choice we can make is whether we are to be good scientists or bad scientists. In her TED talk, science author and philosopher Laura Snyder spoke of how more and more of us are choosing to be bad scientists. Snyder said that only 28% of American adults have even a basic sense of scientific literacy. In her talk, Snyder quoted Charles Darwin's statement, "I sometimes think that general and popular treatises are almost as important for the progress of science as original work."[3]

Snyder added: "Darwin knew what we seem to have forgotten: that science is not only for scientists."[4]

But the rules of producing good science and producing sound beliefs are essentially the same. Both systems require that we adhere to specific processes for evaluating the world. These processes include being openminded to new views; consistently applying our tools of reasoning; being aware of our biases; being thorough when evaluating data and evidence; assuming the good intent behind opposing views; and believing slowly. Above all, we must strive to be skeptical – initially doubting the beliefs not only of others, but of ourselves – and to be aware of the tendency to elevate our own views above the views of others.

END NOTES

Introduction

1. Retrieved July 21, 2020, from https://www.brainyquote.com/quotes/baruch_spinoza_389977.
2. Hitchens, Christopher. (2005). *Letters to a Young Contrarian*. Basic Books.
3. Galilei, Galileo. *Letter to the Grand Duchess Christina*. Retrieved Nov.14, 2020, from https://www.goodreads.com/quotes/2388-i-do-not-feel-obliged-to-believe-that-the-same.
4. Stokes, Philip. (2012) *Philosophy: 100 Essential Thinkers (Loc. 355)*. Arcturus Publishing.

Chapter One

1. Buckley, Theodore Alois. *The Canons and Decrees of the Council of Trent (Illustrated)* Council of Trent, Canon 33. Aeterna Press. Kindle Edition. Literally, "If any one shall say, that, by this Catholic doctrine touching justification, set forth by this holy synod in this present decree, aught is derogated from the glory of God, or the merits of our Lord Jesus Christ, and not rather that the truth of our faith, and the glory in fine of God and of Christ Jesus are rendered illustrious; let him be anathema." Translation retrieved Oct. 25, 2020, from https://carm.org/catholic/council-trent-canons-justification.
2. Harari, Yuval Noah. *Sapiens: A Brief History of Humankind.* (p.280) Vintage.
3. Luther, Martin. Table Talk. Retrieved Oct. 5, 2020, from http://www.astronomy.ohio-state.edu/~pogge/Ast161/Unit3/response.html.
4. Wootton, David. *The Invention of Science: A New History of the Scientific Revolution.* (p. 266) HarperCollins.

Superstition

[1] Voltaire. (2016) *Voltaire - Premium Collection: Novels, Philosophical Writings, Historical Works, Plays, Poems & Letters* . e-artnow. Kindle Edition.

[2] Durant, Will; Durant, Ariel. (1961) *The Age of Reason Begins: The Story of Civilization, Volume VII*. Simon & Schuster.

[3] Cicero, Marcus Tullius. *The Collected Works of Cicero: The Complete Works*. Pergamon Media (Highlights of World Literature). Kindle Edition.

[4] Ingersoll, Robert Green. *The Works of Robert G. Ingersoll, Vol. 1*. Dresden Edition - Lectures. Kindle Edition.

[5] Cooper, James Fenimore. Retrieved Oct. 15, 2020, from https://www.brainyquote.com/quotes/james_fenimore_cooper_204415.

[6] Carrier, Richard. *Sense and Goodness Without God*. Authorhouse. Kindle Edition.

[7] Coyne, Jerry A. (2015) *Faith vs. Fact: Why Science and Religion Are Incompatible*. Penguin Random House.

The Reformation

[1] Luther, Martin. Retrieved Nov. 22, 2020, from https://godinterest.com/2017/12/15/50-profound-martin-luther-quotes-about-faith/.

[2] Livio, Mario. (2020). *Galileo and the Science Deniers*. (p. 9). Simon & Schuster. Kindle Edition.

[3] Russell, Bertrand. *Russell: The Basic Writings of Bertrand Russell* (p. 348). Routledge Classics.

[4] Snyder, Laura J. (2015) *Eye of the Beholder: Johannes Vermeer, Antoni van Leeuwenhoek, and the Reinvention of Seeing*. W.W. Norton & Co.

[5] Durant, Will. (1968) *The Age of Reason Begins: The Story of Civilization, Volume VII*. Simon & Schuster.

[6] Kepler, Johannes. Retrieved Oct. 11, 2020, from https://www.metmuseum.org/blogs/now-at-the-met/2020/alchemy-science-making-marvels.

Chapter Two

1. Diderot, Denis. Retrieved Oct. 20, 2020, from https://euppublishing.com/doi/pdfplus/10.3366/jsp.2016.0136.
2. Sagan, Carl; Druyan, Ann. (1994) *Pale Blue Dot: A Vision of the Human Future in Space*. Ballantine Books.
3. Pianka, Eric. (April 1, 2006). *Doomsday: UT Prof says death is imminent*. The Seguin Gazette-Enterprise. Retrieved Dec. 2, 2020, from https://rense.com/general70/.
4. Darwin, Charles. Retrieved Sept. 12, 2020, from https://www.goodreads.com/quotes/7488031-man-in-his-arrogance-thinks-himself-a-great-work-worthy.
5. Durant, Will. (2011) *On the Meaning of Life*. Literary Licensing. Kindle Edition.

The Centrality of Humans: Anthropomorphism

1. Nietzche, Friedrich. Retrieved Nov. 12, 2020, from https://www.goodreads.com/quotes/87483-is-man-one-of-god-s-blunders-or-is-god-one.
2. Spinoza, Baruch. (2016) *Complete Writing of Spinoza: The Ethics, A Theologico-Political Treatise, On the Improvement of Understanding, Correspondence - Annotated Writing and Life Changing*. Amazon Kindle Edition.
3. Sagan, Carl; Druyan, Ann. (1994) *Pale Blue Dot*. Random House Publishing Group. Kindle Edition.
4. Sagan, Carl; Druyan, Ann. (1994) *Pale Blue Dot*. Random House Publishing Group. Kindle Edition.
5. Darwin, Charles. *Darwin: The Five Essential Works*. Titan Read. Kindle Edition.
6. Darwin, Charles. *Darwin: The Five Essential Works*. Titan Read. Kindle Edition.
7. Dawkins, Richard. (2004) *A Devil's Chaplain: Reflections on Hope, Lies, Science, and Love*. Mariner Books.
8. Goodall, Jane. (2007) Ted Talk. https://www.ted.com/talks/jane_goodall_how_humans_and_animals_can_live_together/transcript.
9. Linder, Douglas O. Retrieved Jan. 5, 2021, from https://famous-trials.com/animalrights/2593-animal-rights-personhood-trials-a-chronology.

[10] Muir, John. Retrieved Oct. 19, 2020, from, https://www.brainyquote.com/quotes/john_muir_752676.
[11] Muir, John. Retrieved Oct. 19, 2020, from https://www.brainyquote.com/quotes/john_muir_752677.
[12] Diamond, Jared. (2006) *The Third Chimpanzee: The Evolution and Future of the Human Animal.* Harper Perennial.

Authority Gets a Demotion

[1] Sagan, Carl. Retrieved Oct. 15, 2020, from https://www.goodreads.com/quotes/7398067-one-of-the-great-commandments-of-science-is-mistrust-arguments.
[2] Livio, Mario. *Galileo and the Science Deniers.* (p. 4) Simon & Schuster, Kindle Edition.
[3] Russell, Bertrand. *A History of Western Philosophy*, Book One. Ancient Philosophy, *Part II. Socrates, Plato and Aristotle, Chapter XXII.* (p. 202) Routlege.
[4] Bruno, Giordano. Retrieved Nov. 18, 2020, from https://www.theosophy.world/resource/quotes/quotes-giordano-bruno.
[5] Ingersoll, Robert Green. *Thomas Paine From The Gods and Other Lectures.* Public Domain. Kindle Edition.
[6] Galilei, Galileo. Letter to Johannes Kepler (1610), as quoted in *The Crime of Galileo* (1955), by Giorgio De Santillana.
[7] Livio, Mario. *Galileo and the Science Deniers.* (p. 235-6). Simon & Schuster, Kindle Edition.
[8] Galilei, Galileo. Retrieved Dec. 1, 2020, from https://www.fossilhunters.xyz/galileo-galilei/how-to-go-to-heaven-not-how-the-heavens-go.html.
[9] Chase, Stuart. Quoted in *Language in Thought and Action* by Samuel Ichiye Hayakawa. Harcourt Publishers.
[10] Einstein, Albert. Retrieved Oct. 27, 2020, from https://www.goodreads.com/quotes/20383-common-sense-is-the-collection-of-prejudices-acquired-by-age.
[11] Stalin, Joseph. Retrieved Jan. 7, 2021, from https://oxford.universitypressscholarship.com/view/10.1093/acprof:osobl/9780195381214.001.0001/acprof-9780195381214-chapter-10.

Chapter Three

1. Russell, Bertrand. Retrieved Dec. 15, 2020, from http://www.blupete.com/Literature/Biographies/Philosophy/Russell.htm.
2. Confucius. *Analects of Confucius.* Book XV Retrieved Dec. 5, 2020, from http://confucius-1.com/analects/analects-15.html.
3. Matthew 7:12.
4. Poincaré, Henri. Retrieved Nov. 28, 2020, from https://todayinsci.com/P/Poincare_Henri/PoincareHenri-Quotations.htm.
5. Gleiser, Marcelo. *Laws of Man and Laws of Nature.* June 26, 2013. NPR. Retrieved Oct 21, 2020, from https://www.npr.org/sections/13.7/2013/06/26/195534987/laws-of-man-and-laws-of-nature.
6. Galilei, Galileo Retrieved Nov. 6, 2020, from https://web.stanford.edu/~jsabol/certainty/readings/Galileo-LetterDuchessChristina.pdf.
7. Poincaré, Henri. *The Foundations of Science: Science and Hypothesis, The Value of Science, Science and Method.* (p. 207) Kindle Edition.
8. Aristotle. *The History of Animals,* Book 2, Part 3. Retrieved Jan. 8, 2020, from http://classics.mit.edu/Aristotle/history_anim.2.ii.html.
9. Russell, Bertrand. (1952) *The Impact of Science on Society.* Routledge Classics.
10. Gailei, Galileo. Retrieved Oct. 22, 2020, from https://www.goodreads.com/quotes/8706545-where-the-senses-fail-us-reason-must-step-in.
11. Wootton, David. (2015) *The Invention of Science: A New History of the Scientific Revolution.* (p. 254) Harper Collins.
12. Gailei, Galileo. Retrieved Oct. 8, 2020, from https://victor-mochere.com/best-quotes-from-galileo-galilei.
13. Wootton, David.(2015) *The Invention of Science: A New History of the Scientific Revolution.* (p. 254) Harper Collins.
14. Huxley, Aldous. *Complete Essays, Vol. II: 1926-1929.* Ivan R. Dee.
15. Picoult, Jodi. (2006) *Keeping the Faith.* Harper Perennial.
16. Donne, John. *The Complete Poems of John Donne.* (p. 135) Neeland Media LLC. Kindle Edition.
17. Collins, Francis. *God vs. Science: A Spirited Debate Between Atheist Biologist Richard Dawkins and Christian Geneticist Francis Collins.*

Time magazine. Retrieved Aug. 16, 2020, from http://inters.org/Dawkins-Collins-Cray-Science. Also in Nov. 13, 2006, issue of Time.
[18] Shermer, Michael (2015) *The Moral Arc: How Science Leads Humanity Toward Truth, Justice, and Freedom.* Henry Holt & Co.
[19] Seneca. Retrieved August 26, 2020, from https://www.goodreads.com/quotes/1034812-religion-is-regarded-by-the-common-people-as-true-by.
[20] De Mello, Anthony. Retrieved July 21, 2020 from https://www.brainyquote.com/quotes/anthony_de_mello_133824
[21] Spinoza, Baruch. *The Ethics, Part IV, Of Human Bondage, or the Strength of Emotions.* Some Good Press. Kindle Edition.
[22] Popper, Karl. (1996) *Myth of the Framework.* (p. 8) Routledge.
[23] Faraday, Michael. (1859) "Experimental Researches in Chemistry and Physics", p.471. London, R. Taylor and W. Francis.
[24] Kepler, Johannes. Retrieved Oct. 1, 2020, from http://www.nmsciencefoundation.org/quotes.htm.
[25] Galilei, Galileo. Retrieved Nov. 14, 2020, from, https://www.goodreads.com/quotes/41204-measure-what-can-be-measured-and-make-measurable-what-cannot.
[26] Spinoza, Baruch. *Theological-Political Treatise.* Hackett Publishing Co.
[27] Durant, Will. *Story of Philosophy.* (p. 16) Simon & Schuster. Kindle Edition.

Chapter Four

[1] Bacon, Francis. (2015) *Novum Organum.* Centaur Editions.
[2] Russell, Bertrand. Retrieved Aug. 7, 2020, from https://www.goodreads.com/quotes/172227-it-is-not-what-the-man-of-science-believes-that, also *Religion and Science* audiobook.
[3] Tyson, Neil deGrasse. Retrieved June 9, 2020, from https://www.goodreads.com/quotes/340727-the-good-thing-about-science-is-that-it-s-true-whether.
[4] Minchin, Tim. Commencement Address, University of Australia. Retrieved Jun. 29, 2020, from https://genius.com/Tim-minchin-commencement-speech-and-university-of-western-australia-annotated.

[5] Russell, Bertrand. Retrieved June 30, 2020, from http://www.quotationspage.com/quote/32856.html.
[6] Sagan, Carl. (1996) *The Demon-Haunted World: Science as a Candle in the Dark*. Ballantine Books.
[7] Bacon, Francis. (2015) *Novum Organum*. Centaur Editions.
[8] Santayana, George. Retrieved Dec. 4, 2020, from https://quotepark.com/quotes/931595-george-santayana-skepticism-like-chastity-should-not-be-relinquis/.
[9] Montaigne, Michel. *An Apology for Raymond Sebond*. Penguin Classics.
[10] Paul, Richard; Elder, Linda. *The Miniature Guide to the Art of Asking Essential Questions*. Foundation for Critical Thinking Press. Kindle Edition.
[11] Galilei, Galileo. Retrieved Dec. 10, 2020, from https://www.brilliantread.com/51-famous-galileo-galilei-quotes-thoughts-and-advice/.
[12] Harari, Yuval Noah. *Sapiens: A Brief History of Humankind*. (p. 279) Vintage.
[13] Popper, Karl. Retrieved Dec. 21, 2020, from https://www.goodreads.com/author/quotes/349707.Karl_Popper.
[14] Hume, David. Retrieved Nov. 8, 2020, from https://bestofquotesblog.wordpress.com/2015/09/04/david-hume-great-quotes/.
[15] Durant, Ariel; Durant, Will. (1968)*The Lessons of History*. Simon and Schuster.
[16] Sagan, Carl. Retrieved June 9, 2020, from https://www.goodreads.com/quotes/459665-there-are-many-hypotheses-in-science-that-are-wrong-that-s.
[17] Oreskes, Naomi. (2019) *Why Trust Science?* (The University Center for Human Values Series) (p. 31). Princeton University Press. Kindle Edition.
[18] Livio, Mario. *Galileo and the Science Deniers* (p. 157). Simon & Schuster. Kindle Edition.
[19] Harari, Yuval Noah. *Sapiens: A Brief History of Humankind*. (p. 281) Vintage.
[20] Feynman, Richard. (1974) Caltech commencement address, 1974. *Cargo Cult Science*. Retrieved Dec. 21, 2020, from https://sites.cs.ucsb.edu/~ravenben/cargocult.html.
[21] Pirsig, Robert *Zen and the Art of Motorcycle Maintenance: An*

Inquiry into Values. William Morrow Paperbacks.
22. Darwin, Charles. *More Letters of Charles Darwin, Vol 2.* Public Domain.
23. Huxley, Thomas. *The Progress of Science.* Retrieved Dec. 27, 2020, from http://homes.chass.utoronto.ca/~ian/huxley2.htm.
24. Hodgell, P.C. *The Seekers Mask.* Meisha Merlin Publishing.
25. Carrier, Richard. (2005) *Sense and Goodness Without God.* Authorhouse. Kindle Edition.

Chapter Five

1. Asimov, Isaac. Retrieved Nov. 19, 2020, from https://libquotes.com/isaac-asimov/quote/lbv3a8r.
2. McIntyre, Lee. (2019) *The Scientific Attitude: Defending Science from Denial, Fraud, and Pseudoscience.* MIT Press.
3. Feynman, Richard P. Retrieved Sept. 25, 2020, from *https://www.goodreads.com/quotes/1134331-i-would-rather-have-questions-that-can-t-be-answered-than*. BBC Horizon Interview.
4. Dumas, Jean-Baptiste. Retrieved Sept. 21, 2020, from https://thefactfactor.com/facts/pure_science/physics/scientific-method/11712/.
5. Carrier, Richard. *(2005) Sense and Goodness Without God* Authorhouse. Kindle Edition.
6. Popper, Karl. Retrieved July 28, 2020, from https://www.blackstonetutors.co.uk/bmat-section-3-question-types.html.
7. Popper, Karl (1965) Retrieved Nov. 19, 2020, from https://www.angelfire.com/country/palestine/compareandcontrast.htm.
8. McIntyre, Lee. (2019) *The Scientific Attitude: Defending Science from Denial, Fraud, and Pseudoscience* (p. 33) MIT Press.
9. Fermi, Enrico. Retrieved July 17, 2020, from https://todayinsci.com/F/Fermi_Enrico/FermiEnrico-Quotations.htm.
10. Rowling, J.K. Retrieved June 18, 2020, from https://www.goodreads.com/quotes/76664-i-mean-you-could-claim-that-anything-s-real-if-the.
11. Russell, Bertrand. Retrieved Oct. 20, 2020, from https://rationalwiki.org/wiki/Russell%27s_Teapot. Unpublished article.

[12] Paine, Thomas. *Thomas Paine : Collected Writings : Common Sense / The American Crisis / The Rights of Man / The Age of Reason / A Letter Addressed to the Abbe Raynal.* Coyote Canyon Press. Kindle Edition.

[13] Ball, W.W.Rouse. Quotes Laplace in *A Short Account of the History of Mathematics* Retrieved Nov. 27, 2020, from https://www.maths.tcd.ie/pub/HistMath/People/Laplace/RouseBall/RB_Laplace.html.

[14] Carrier, Richard (2005) *Sense and Goodness Without God.* Authorhouse. Kindle Edition.

[15] Asimov, Isaac. *Cult of Ignorance.* Newsweek. Jan. 21,1980.

[16] Novella, Stephen. *Your Deceptive Mind: A Scientific Guide to Critical Thinking Skills.* The Great Courses.

[17] Novella, Stephen. *Your Deceptive Mind: A Scientific Guide to Critical Thinking Skills.* The Great Courses.

[18] Ingersoll, Robert Green. Retrieved July 9, 2020, from https://www.brainyquote.com/quotes/robert_green_ingersoll_719062.

[19] Popper, Karl. Retrieved Sept. 6, 2020, from https://www.azquotes.com/quote/584241.

[20] de Montaigne, Michel. (1580) *The Essays: Michel de Montaigne.* Pandora's Boy Classics. Kindle Edition.

[21] Bacon, Francis. *The Collected Works of Sir Francis Bacon.* Halcyon Press. Kindle Edition.

[22] Anonymous. Retrieved July 20, 2020, from https://www.goodreads.com/quotes/48955-when-the-debate-is-lost-slander-becomes-the-tool-of.

[23] Chris Jami. (2018) *Healology.*
Kindle Edition.

[24] Weaver, Aaron. *What Is QAnon? Here Are 5 Core Beliefs of the Shocking Conspiracy Theory.* CNN (July 26, 2020) Retrieved Dec. 8, 2020, from https://www.ccn.com/what-is-qanon-conspiracy-theory.

[25] Sinclair, Upton. *I, Candidate for Governor and How I Got Licked.* University of California Press (December 16, 1994).

[26] Diderot, Denis. Retrieved Dec. 23, 2020, from https://www.reddit.com/r/MensRights/comments/6vhdgi/denis_diderot_171384_all_things_must_be_examined/.

[27] Wilson, Robert Anton. *Prometheus Rising.* Hilaritas Press.

[28] Stokes, DeShanne. Retrieved Feb. 8, 2021, from https://

www.goodreads.com/quotes/8303508-truth-is-hard-propaganda-is-cheap.

[29] Franken, Al. Retrieved Oct. 13, 2020, from https://quotesgram.com/quote/al-franken/465114-the-biases-the-media-has-are-much-bigger.

[30] Murrow, Edward R. Retrieved July 1, 2020, from https://www.goodreads.com/quotes/39015-our-major-obligation-is-not-to-mistake-slogans-for-solutions.

[31] Tang, Davie. Retrieved July 19, 2020, from https://www.inspiringquotes.us/quotes/Qyuw_9XrOgKFP.

[32] Boorstein, Sylvia. Retrieved Dec. 21, 2020, from https://www.goodreads.com/quotes/951578-the-mind-is-like-tofu-it-tastes-like-whatever-you.

[33] McIntyre, Lee. (2019) *The Scientific Attitude: Defending Science from Denial, Fraud, and Pseudoscience.* (p. 152) MIT Press.

[34] Orwell, George. Retrieved Apr. 25, 2020, from https://www.orwellfoundation.com/the-orwell-youth-prize/2018-youth-prize/previous-winners-youth/2016-winners/if-liberty-means-anything-at-all-it-means-the-right-to-tell-people-what-they-do-not-want-to-hear-alexander-butcher/.

[35] Carole Cadwalladr. *Facebook is Out of Control. If It Were a Country It Would Be North Korea.* The Guardian. (July 5, 2020) Retrieved Jan. 5, 2020, from https://www.theguardian.com/technology/2020/jul/05/facebook-is-out-of-control-if-it-were-a-country-it-would-be-north-korea.

[36] Thompson, Clive. *YouTube's Plot to Silence Conspiracy Theories.* Wired. (Sept. 18, 2020).

[37] Becker, Joseph Raphael. *Annabelle & Aiden: Oh, the Things We Believed!* Imaginarium Press.

[38] Jung, Carl. Retrieved Sept.19, 2020, from https://carljungdepthpsychologysite.blog/2020/07/23/carl-jung-in-all-chaos-there-is-a-cosmos-in-all-disorder-a-secret-order/#.X-p3gi2cbJI.

[39] Kierkegaard, Søren. Retrieved June 4, 2020, from https://www.goodreads.com/quotes/35782-there-are-two-ways-to-be-fooled-one-is-to.

[40] Huxley, Thomas. Retrieved Nov. 29, 2020, from https://www.classicsnetwork.com/quotes/authors/Huxley.

[41] Twain, Mark. Retrieved April 2, 2020, from https://

www.goodreads.com/quotes/633116-there-has-been-much-tragedy-in-my-life-at-least.

42. Sapolsky, Robert. *Robert Sapolsky Discusses Physiological Effects of Stress* from https://news.stanford.edu/news/2007/march7/sapolskysr-030707.html. Stanford News. (March 7, 2007).

43. Ehrlich, Paul. *Stanford Researcher Declares that the Sixth Mass Extinction Is Here*. From https://news.stanford.edu/2015/06/19/mass-extinction-ehrlich-061915/. Stanford News. (Jun. 19, 2015)

44. Hume, David. *A Treatise of Human Nature*. Kindle Version.

45. Russell, Bertrand. (1928) *The Recrudescence of Puritanism, in Sceptical Essays*. Routlege.

46. Bekoff, Mark. Retrieved Oct. 6, 2020, from https://www.goodreads.com/quotes/tag/anecdote.

47. Paine, Thomas. *Thomas Paine: Collected Writings: Common Sense / The American Crisis / The Rights of Man / The Age of Reason / A Letter Addressed to the Abbe Raynal*. Coyote Canyon Press. Kindle Edition.

48. Gervais, Ricky. Retrieved Dec. 30, 2020, from https://www.azquotes.com/quote/575591?ref=burden-of-proof.

49. Besant, Annie. Retrieved Nov. 24, 2020, from https://www.azquotes.com/quotes/topics/burden-of-proof.html.

50. Burns, Robert. *Collected Poems of Robert Burns*. Wordsworth Editions. First Edition.

51. "Futurama." Episode: *A Clockwork Origin*." S06E09. Retrieved Jan. 15, 2021, from https://transcripts.fandom.com/wiki/Futurama.

52. McCallister, Nathan. *Proportionality Bias: The Hidden Driver of Conspiracy Theories*. Retrieved July 22, 2020, from https://medium.com/@nathanmccallister/proportionality-bias-the-hidden-driver-of-conspiracy-theories-fa13401a7373.

53. Sternheiner, Karen. *The Sociology of Conspiracy* Everyday Sociology Blog. (Sept.26, 2007) https://www.everydaysociologyblog.com/page/115/.

54. Hawley, Noah. Retrieved Aug. 16, 2020, from https://www.brainyquote.com/quotes/noah_hawley_874476.

55. Dickey, Colin. *How to Talk to a Conspiracy Theorist* Retrieved Oct. 7, 2020, from https://gen.medium.com/how-to-talk-to-a-conspiracy-theorist-20122a39ac8a.

56. Sagan. Carl. (Dec. 14, 1980). "Encyclopaedia Galactica." *Cosmos: A Personal Voyage*. Episode 12. At mark of 1 minute 24 seconds. PBS.
57. Nichols, Thomas M. (2018) *The Death of Expertise: The Campaign Against Established Knowledge and Why it Matters*. Oxford University Press. Kindle Edition.
58. Popper, Karl. Retrieved June 9, 2020, from https://www.goodreads.com/quotes/165784-no-rational-argument-will-have-a-rational-effect-on-a.
59. Nichols, Tom. *The Death of Expertise: The Campaign Against Established Knowledge and Why it Matters*. (p. 3) Oxford University Press.
60. Popper, Karl. As quoted by Mark Damazer in *In Our Time's Greatest Philosopher Vote* on "In Our Time" (BBC 4). From https://quotes.yourdictionary.com/author/karl-popper/.
61. Kundera, Milan.(1999) *Laughable Loves*. Harper Perennial.
62. O'Rourke, P.J. Retrieved Jan. 7, 2020, from https://www.brainyquote.com/quotes/p_j_orourke_106010.
63. McLuhan, Marshall. (1970) *Culture Is Our Business*. (p. 66) Wipf and Stock. Reprint Edition (Feb. 12, 2015).
64. Becket, Stefan; Quinn, Melissa; Segers, Grace; Linton, Caroline. *2020 Election "most secure in history," Security Officials Say*. CBSNews.com. Retrieved Nov 13, 2020, from https://www.cbsnews.com/live-updates/2020-election-most-secure-history-dhs/.
65. The Washington Post Retrieved Jan. 25, 2021, from https://www.washingtonpost.com/politics/trump-raffensperger-call-transcript-georgia-vote/2021/01/03/2768e0cc-4ddd-11eb-83e3-322644d82356_story.html.
66. Wise, Alana. *Trump Fires Election Security Director Who Corrected Voter Fraud Disinformation*. National Public Radio. Nov. 17, 2020. Retrieved from https://www.npr.org/2020/11/17/936003057/cisa-director-chris-krebs-fired-after-trying-to-correct-voter-fraud-disinformati.
67. "Armed Protesters Flock to Michigan Official's Home." Dec.20, 2020. BBC, from https://www.bbc.com/news/election-us-2020-55220570.
68. Moye, David. *Trump Attorney Mocked For Demanding Biden Prove Trump's Fraud Claims*. (Nov. 12, 2020). Huffington Post.

Retrieved Dec. 16, 2020, from https://www.huffpost.com/entry/jenna-ellis-biden-prove-trump-fraud-claims_n_5fad8096c5b6ed84597f67c4.

[69] Cook, Tim, "International Data Privacy Day" speech on Jan 30, 2021. As quoted in *Tim Cook May Have Just Ended Facebook: Looks Like It's No More Mr. Nice Guy*, by Justin Bariso. Inc Magazine. (Jan 30, 2021). From https://www.inc.com/justin-bariso/tim-cook-may-have-just-ended-facebook.html.

Chapter Seven

[1] Allen, Ethan. Retrieved February 15, 2020, from https://www.brainyquote.com/quotes/ethan_allen_193074?src=t_reason.

[2] Spinoza, Baruch. *Complete Writings of Spinoza: The Ethics, A Theologico-Political Treatise, On the Improvement of Understanding, Correspondence - Annotated Writing and Life Changing.* Kindle Edition.

[3] Haidt, Jonathan. (2012) *The Righteous Mind: Why Good People Are Divided by Politics and Religion.* (p. 366) Vintage.

[4] Huxley, Aldous. Retrieved Nov. 2, 2020 from https://www.goodreads.com/quotes/94619-the-propagandist-s-purpose-is-to-make-one-set-of-people.

[5] Rilke, Rainer Maria. "I Live My Life in Widening Circles" from *Rilke's Book of Hours: Love Poems to God.* Riverhead Books.

[6] Swift, Jonathan Retrieved Dec. 19, 2020, from https://quoteinvestigator.com/2015/07/10/reason-out/.

[7] Spinoza Baruch.*Theological-Political Treatise.* Kindle Edition.

[8] Twain, Mark. Retrieved Nov. 22, 2020, from https://www.goodreads.com/quotes/584507-it-s-easier-to-fool-people-than-to-convince-them-that.

[9] Feynman, Richard. (1974) *Cargo Cult Science* from https://sites.cs.ucsb.edu/~ravenben/cargocult.html.

[10] Jillette, Penn. Retrieved Oct. 28, 2020, from https://www.goodreads.com/author/quotes/134143.Penn_Jillette.

[11] Hume, David. *David Hume: 21 Works.* Unknown. Kindle Edition.

[12] Russell, Bertrand. *Unpopular Essays.* Routledge Classics.

[13] Shakespeare, William. *Troilus and Cressida* (Act II Scene 2). Public Domain Kindle Edition.

14. Durant, Will. *On the Meaning of Life*. Promethean Press. Kindle Edition.
15. Wordsworth, William Retrieved Dec. 20, 2020, from https://www.brainyquote.com/quotes/william_wordsworth_120837.
16. Russell, Bertrand. *Free Thought and Official Propaganda*. Transcript. Kindle Edition.
17. René Descartes. Retrieved Dec. 1, 2020, from https://www.goodreads.com/quotes/28930-if-you-would-be-a-real-seeker-after-truth-it.
18. Bacon, Francis. *The Collected Works of Sir Francis Bacon* (Unexpurgated Edition). Halcyon Press. Kindle Edition.
19. Sinclair, Upton. Retrieved Dec. 24, 2020, from https://www.azquotes.com/quote/1389614.
20. Clifford, William Kingdon. *The Ethics of Belief* (Illustrated). (p. 15) Kindle Edition.
21. Gandhi, Mohandas K. Retrieved Nov. 17, 2020, from https://sectionpoems.wordpress.com/2012/12/17/mahatma-gandhi-a-man-is-but-the-product-of-his-thoughts-what-he-thinks-he-becomes/.
22. Voltaire. Retrieved June 9, 2020, from https://www.goodreads.com/quotes/20527-those-who-can-make-you-believe-absurdities-can-make-you.
23. Santayana, George. *The Essential George Santayana Collection* (Unexpurgated Edition). Halcyon Press. Kindle Edition.
24. Santayana, George. *The Complete Works of George Santayana*. Shrine of Knowledge. Kindle Edition.
25. Hardy, Darren. Retrieved Jan. 9, 2021, from https://www.azquotes.com/quote/1497926.
26. Clifford, William Kingdon. *The Ethics of Belief (Illustrated)*. (p. 20) Kindle Edition.
27. McIntyre, Lee (2019) *The Scientific Attitude: Defending Science from Denial, Fraud, and Pseudoscience*. (p 151) MIT Press.
28. Clifford, William Kingdon. *The Ethics of Belief (Illustrated)*. (p. 19). Kindle Edition.
29. Smirconish, Michael. *Things I Wish I Knew Before I Started Talking*. CNN Press Room.
30. Wittgenstein, Ludwig. Retrieved Oct. 5, 2020, from https://www.goodreads.com/quotes/259093-this-is-how-philosophers-should-salute-each-other-take-your.

[31] Aurelius, Marcus. *Meditations - Stoics In Their Own Words Book 2* (Enhanced Edition (Illustrated. Newly revised text. Includes Image Gallery + Audio). (p. 30) Enhanced Media. Kindle Edition.

[32] Diderot, Denis. Retrieved Oct. 5, 2020, from https://www.goodreads.com/quotes/7361887-it-is-very-important-not-to-mistake-hemlock-for-parsley.

[33] Twain, Mark Retrieved Apr. 31, 2020, from https://www.goodreads.com/quotes/234445-the-less-there-is-to-justify-a-traditional-custom-the.

[34] Livio, Mario. (2015) *Galileo and the Science Deniers*. (p 86) Simon & Schuster. Kindle Edition.

[35] Popper, Karl. Retrieved Dec. 4, 2020, from https://www.azquotes.com/quote/1268891.

[36] Hitchens, Christopher. Retrieved Nov. 28, 2020, from https://internetpoem.com/christopher-hitchens/quotes/.

[37] Livio, Mario. (2015) *Galileo and the Science Deniers*. (p. 96) Simon & Schuster. Kindle Edition.

[38] Patterson, Kerry; Patterson, Kerry; Grenny, Joseph; Grenny, Joseph; McMillan, Ron; McMillan, Ron; Switzler, Al; Switzler, Al. *Crucial Conversations Tools for Talking When Stakes Are High*. (Second Edition). (p. 23) McGraw-Hill Education. Kindle Edition.

[39] Clarke, Arthur C. Retrieved Dec. 5, 2020, from https://quoteinvestigator.com/2017/03/24/astrology/.

[40] Minchin, Timothy. *Commencement Speech, University of Western Australia*. From https://genius.com/Tim-minchin-commencement-speech-and-university-of-western-australia-annotated.

[41] Bacon, Francis. *Francis Bacon: The Complete Works* (Centaur Classics). Kindle Edition.

[42] Ionessco, Eugene. Retrieved Nov. 7, 2020, from https://philosiblog.com/2012/06/01/it-is-not-the-answer-that-enlightens-but-the-question/.

[43] Paul, Richard; Elder, Linda. *The Miniature Guide to The Art of Asking Essential Questions*. Foundation for Critical Thinking. Kindle Edition.

[44] Rusk, Dean. Retrieved Dec. 12, 2020, from https://www.airuniversity.af.edu/Portals/10/AFNC/dispute-

45. Stone, Douglas. (2010) *Difficult Conversations: How to Discuss What Matters Most.* Penguin Books.
46. Covey, Steven. Retrieved Dec. 30, 2020, from https://www.franklincovey.com/the-7-habits/habit-5/.
47. Sagan, Carl. *Demon-Haunted World: Science as a Candle in the Dark.* Random House Publishing Group. Kindle Edition.
48. Phillip E. Johnson Quotes. (n.d.). BrainyQuote.com. Retrieved March 4, 2021, from BrainyQuote.com Web site: https://www.brainyquote.com/quotes/phillip_e_johnson_288758.
49. Jackson, Robert. Retrieved Nov. 6, 2020 from https://www.brainyquote.com/quotes/robert_jackson_200896.
50. Shapin, Steven; Schaffer, Simon. (1985) *Leviathan and the Air-Pump: Hobbes, Boyle, and the Experimental Life.* (p. 332) Princeton University Press. Kindle Edition.
51. Dawkins, Richard. Retrieved June 12, 2020, from https://www.brainyquote.com/quotes/richard_dawkins_626775.
52. Pinker, Stephen. (1994) *The Language Instinct: How the Mind Creates Language.* Audible Version.
53. Wittgenstein, Ludwig. Retrieved June 12, 2020, from https://www.goodreads.com/quotes/12577-the-limits-of-my-language-means-the-limits-of-my.
54. Wootton, David. (2015) *The Invention of Science: A New History of the Scientific Revolution.* (p. 48) HarperCollins.

Everything is an Experiment

1. Brockman, John. (2012) *This Will Make You Smarter: New Scientific Concepts to Improve Your Thinking* Harper. Perennial.
2. Sagan, Carl. *Demon-Haunted World: Science as a Candle in the Dark.* Random House Publishing Group. Kindle Edition.
3. Snyder, Laura. TED talk Retrieved Dec.1, 2020 from https://symbionticism.blogspot.com/2013/04/the-history-of-science-when-was-word.html.
4. Snyder, Laura. (2012) *Philosophical Breakfast Club* TED talk. Retrieved Jan. 5, 2021, at https://www.ted.com/talks/laura_snyder_the_philosophical_breakfast_club/transcript.

Share your thoughts by signing up at Good Reasons (www.goodreasons.co)

ACKNOWLEDGEMENTS

Thank you to my primary editor, Dale Ulland. Thank you also to June Hankins for her thoughtful editing and feedback, and also to Valerie Carroll and Tom Lundstrom for feedback on early drafts. Finally, a special thank you goes to the many great thinkers throughout history who have passed down their wisdom so that every generation does not have to start from scratch trying to figure out how our minds work.

Gil Carroll lives in Centennial, Colorado.

www.ingramcontent.com/pod-product-compliance
Lightning Source LLC
Chambersburg PA
CBHW020907080526
44589CB00011B/480